The Practice of Generalist Case Management

The Practice of Generalist Case Management

Barbara J. Holt
West Virginia University

Allyn and Bacon

Boston ▪ London ▪ Toronto ▪ Sydney ▪ Tokyo ▪ Singapore

Senior Series Editor, Social Work and Family Therapy: *Judy Fifer*
Editor-in-Chief, Social Sciences: *Karen Hanson*
Series Editorial Assistant: *Julianna M. Cancio*
Marketing Manager: *Jackie Aaron*
Production Editor: *Christopher H. Rawlings*
Editorial-Production Service: *Omegatype Typography, Inc.*
Composition and Prepress Buyer: *Linda Cox*
Manufacturing Buyer: *Julie McNeill*
Cover Administrator: *Jenny Hart*
Electronic Composition: *Omegatype Typography, Inc.*

Copyright © 2000 by Allyn & Bacon
A Pearson Education Company
160 Gould Street
Needham Heights, MA 02494

Internet: www.abacon.com

Library of Congress Cataloging-in-Publication Data

Holt, Barbara J.
    The practice of generalist case management / Barbara J. Holt
        p.   cm.
    Includes bibliographical references (p.   ) and index.
    ISBN 0-205-28733-6 (pbk.)
    1. Social case work—Management.   2. Social work administration.   I. Title.
HV43.H64   2000
361.3'2—dc21
                                                                    99-34804
                                                                       CIP

Printed in the United States of America

10 9 8 7 6 5 4 3 2 1   04 03 02 01 00 99

Dedicated to the memory of Sheila Oxley,
who perfected the role of case manager and best friend.

CONTENTS

PREFACE

Case management has become so popular so fast because it addresses the two issues dearest to the hearts of Americans: It promotes freedom, and it saves money. Almost all proposals for health care reform contain some case management components. Most social service agencies have professionals performing case management tasks, either exclusively or as part of a larger role. Mental health services utilize case managers to assist clients in adjusting to life in the community, and criminal justice case managers seek to make community placement safe for the client and society.

From the years I have spent designing, implementing, and administering case management programs and training those who perform as case managers, I have learned that there is no single source of the "perfect" case manager. From social workers to music majors, from registered nurses to accountants, it has been the characteristics of commitment and the enthusiasm that produced the exceptional case manager. The desire to go the extra step in the client's best interest, to listen patiently to stories already heard, to push for additional services or benefits, and to represent the agency proudly—these are not specific to a particular discipline but to a strong character and sense of confidence.

I have also learned that, regardless of academic background, few beginning case managers have more than a passing knowledge of the tasks and responsibilities that come with the job. This realization resulted in the creation of a basic training program to establish a foundation of the processes and procedures connected to the role. In addition, because of the varied backgrounds of the case managers, it was necessary to fill in the gaps with information on target populations, caregivers, and outside resources as well as to develop skills in interviewing and negotiation. This comprehensive training received the 1994 Health Care Financing Administration Certificate of Merit.

This text is the result of the ten-year-long development of that training. It is designed for entry-level case managers or those planning on entering the profession so that they may understand the tasks and skills required for effective care of the client population. The case examples included are all real. The inventive solutions by case managers are also true and a continuing source of pride. The less-than-successful outcomes are actual as well and serve to teach us all that case management will always be a challenging and, at times, frustrating method of providing care to those who could not function without us.

Acknowledgments

I would like to offer special thanks to the following colleagues who reviewed either the prospectus or the manuscript for this book: Carol J. Bridges, East Central

University; Elizabeth Cramer, Virginia Commonwealth University; Charles Garvin, University of Michigan; Karen Hopkins, Syracuse University; Rosalie A. Kane, University of Minnesota; Philip McCallion, State University of New York at Albany; and Eleanor D. Tolson, University of Illinois at Chicago.

B.J.H.

ABOUT THE AUTHOR

Barbara J. Holt, PhD, assumed the role of associate director of the Community Service & Outreach Unit in July 1996. Prior to this she was a Policy Fellow at the Health Resources Study Center at the Naval Postgraduate School in Monterey, California, where she designed a case management system at a continuing care retirement community on a closed military base.

Dr. Holt served for ten years as the director of long-term care services for the Alabama Commission on Aging, where she created and implemented health service initiatives for the elderly, including the Governor's Task Force on Long Term Care Reform and the statewide Home and Community-Based Services Program for which she was awarded the 1994 Health Care Financing Administration Certificate of Merit.

Dr. Holt has also taught graduate and undergraduate courses in health policy at West Virginia University, Golden Gate University, and Auburn University, Montgomery. She holds a master of education in counseling from Auburn University, a master of social work from the University of Alabama, and a doctor of philosophy degree from Auburn University in public policy.

The Practice of Generalist Case Management

1 The Origin of the Species

Developing a New Discipline

Although its beginnings actually occur earlier in the delivering of human services, case management as a distinct and popular form of service exploded in the 1980s. Responding to a dysfunctional service delivery system, **case management** attempted to redirect the focus and decision power from the providers and professionals to the clients themselves.[1] A term that was unknown had suddenly become the common element in health care, social work, criminal justice, even auto repair. Each of these fields provided services to a complex population over an extended period of time, often at a high financial and personal cost. Each was searching for a way to provide care in a humane yet cost effective way.

The practice of case management has further evolved in the 1990s with the dramatic changes in health care, particularly the growth of managed care (not to be confused with case management) in both private health maintenance organizations and public programs such as Medicaid and Medicare. Where once the role of the case manager was to find care at a reasonable cost, it has now sometimes become the job of seeking care at any cost. Always tending toward an advocacy role, in some cases the case manager has become a champion of the underserved. Its role in the education and empowerment of the patient as well as its proactive and preventative nature have increased.

Defining Case Management

Case management is based on the principle that a trusting and empowering direct relationship between the case manager and the client is essential to expedite the client's use of services along a continuum of care and to restore or maintain independent functioning to the fullest degree possible. Case management is usually a long-term relationship. Since case management serves those individuals whose disabilities are severe and chronic, case relationships may last years rather than days or weeks.

Case management is multidimensional.

■ *It is direct and indirect.* It incorporates two central functions: providing individual advice, counseling, and therapy to clients in the community and linking clients to needed services and supports in community agencies and informal helping networks. The case manager must have the capacity to provide assistance in a sensitive and supportive manner to particular client populations based on knowledge of human behavior and well-developed observational and communication skills. With this foundation a case manager establishes helping relationships, assesses complex problems, selects problem-solving interventions, and helps clients to function effectively and thus is a therapeutic process. Case management also takes the position that case managers avoid doing those tasks that the client is capable of doing, so that independence and self-esteem are maximized.[2]

■ *It is micro and macro.* Many of the activities of a case manager that are designed to advocate care for an individual also improve care for a caseload or the total client population.

■ *It is vertical and horizontal.* Boundary spanning is essential in providing care across the continuum.[3] Case management must be cross-sectional so that services are comprehensive in order to meet the client's diverse requirements at any one time. Broad attention is required by the multiple needs in the client's life situation. It must also be longitudinal, necessitating that the system continue to provide assistance over time for a changing spectrum of needs.[4]

Social Work's Roots

Social work case management is clearly linked to social case work—a fundamental concept of social work practice. It has its origins in the earliest history of social work practice and the social work profession. All aspects of social work case management rest on a body of established social work knowledge, technical expertise, and humanistic values that allows for the provision of a specialized and unique service to designated client groups. Case management encompasses well-established social work concepts and techniques as an approach to arranging and coordinating care. Traditional social caseworkers maintained a dual focus on the client and the environment, working directly with and indirectly on behalf of individual clients and families in need of social services.

The view of the case manager is not only of the client—his or her physical and mental condition—but also of the environment in which the client functions. Cognizant of the impact of the many elements of the social system in which the client operates, the case manager considers how environmental changes will impact the well-being of the client and, sometimes, how changes in the client's condition will affect his immediate environment. Further, the case manager attempts to modify, cushion, accelerate, or monitor changes from both sides in order to create a safe and stable system.

Not all of the case manager tasks focus on outside intervention to the environment; a frequent role is to educate and support clients as they learn to deal with the social system alone. Such skills not only improve current problems but divert future ones.[5]

Whom Does the Case Manager Serve?

From outside the system, it appears very clear: The client applies or is assigned to a particular case manager and, while the relationship is in force, the case manager takes actions and makes decisions based on the client's best interest. But in actuality, it is seldom that simple and clear cut. Because the client is part of a system, any protective or harmful action that occurs may have implications for those associated in some way. We can divide the players into three groups.

The Payers

Payers are those agencies or companies that have financial outlay so that the client will receive services. Sometimes this payment includes the reimbursement for case management as well as health or social services. The payers such as health plans, insurers, employers, and government payers like Medicaid and Medicare have expectations of receiving a service of approximately the same value as the payment they are making. Many times this includes the expectation of an outcome that relieves them of continuing to pay by either solving the problem so that the client can function without assistance or, at least, shifting them (and their cost) to another payer.

The Clients

The **client** is usually thought of as the individual whose name is on the application forms. However, the experienced case manager knows that family members, especially the primary caregiver, can be the ones who are most in need of assistance and whose wishes must be taken into account. The clients expect excellent care and active participation in the decision-making process.

The Providers

The health care delivery system—clinicians, hospitals, and other organizations and individuals providing care across the continuum—expect case managers to be a bridge between themselves and the other payers and clients. Facing resource depletion, **providers** often look to case management agencies to advocate on behalf of the client to the payers so they may provide care. They may also anticipate the case manager handling issues of conflict with the clients and acting as an intermediary to explain procedures, eligibility requirements, documents, or decisions of the organization.

Why Has Case Management Become Popular?

The significant attention case management currently enjoys is the result of a number of factors.

- First, there is a universality in the approach; the process of evaluation, planning, and implementation are common steps in the solving of any problem and therefore enable it to be used with a wide range of clients.
- Second, the intervention techniques of case management are readily transferable to other professions because they are based on sound, logical, and systematic processes.
- Third, the skills required for case management may be acquired by training and do not require a preexisting base of knowledge in a particular field. Therefore, case managers may have backgrounds in social work, nursing, family and child development, criminal justice, public health, and (some actual cases) accounting and music education. Each discipline brings its own perspective, each population served creates its own demands, but the principles remain stable.
- Fourth, the activities and successes of case management are observable and measurable. The scheduling of services, monitoring of the client, procurement of resources and all the other tasks that case managers perform are easily tracked. Combining this tangible good with the likelihood that there is a fiscal measurement demonstrating a lower cost and/or higher effectiveness in programs that feature case management make it an attractive component.
- Fifth, case management has been accepted politically because it is seen as a modification, rather than a reform of the existing system of care. Establishing new programs, especially by the government, often attracts attention and serves to polarize support. By simply organizing existing service delivery systems from a varied approach, no flags are raised.[6]
- Finally, case management is based on environmental system theory which acknowledges the influence the setting has on the individual.

Focusing on the interaction of the client with the environment, as shown in Figure 1.1, case managers recognize how the environment affects the client's mental and physical status in both positive and negative ways. They also see how the client's behavior and abilities have an effect on the environment. This ecological approach has become fundamental for all social work practice but is best exemplified in the practice of case management. Case managers quickly learn that they cannot create a plan of care and implement it in a vacuum. A problem in any of the environmental factors shown in Figure 1.1 may have serious implications for the effectiveness of services and perhaps even the safety of the client. Table 1.1 shows several examples.

FIGURE 1.1   The Resources and Threats in a Client's Environment

Another feature of the environmental approach is that it focuses on the person–environment relationship rather than placing blame. It also acknowledges the influence of the individual on the environment (see Table 1.2).

Therefore, the client is seen as an equal element in the overall system and not as simply a victim of circumstances. Individual behavior is not excused because of the environment.[7] Understanding these relationships is an integral part of the assessment process.

What a Case Manager Does

Once the social work case manager has identified and engaged clients as a result of outreach or referral activities, he or she conducts a face to face comprehensive assessment with each client. An assessment is designed to determine a client's

TABLE 1.1   Environmental Impacts on Client

Environmental Problem	Affects the Client by
An unreliable primary caregiver	leaving the client alone without sufficient food.
The lack of available medical care	having illnesses go untreated.
The lack of sufficient income	having to choose between medication, food, or heating.
Neighborhood crime	creating fear of leaving the house or sleeping.
Affordable housing	living in unclean or unsafe surroundings.

TABLE 1.2   Client Impact on Environment

Client Characteristics	Affects the Environment by
Bad temper and irritable behavior	keeping friends and neighbors at a distance.
Embarrassment of needing assistance	community services are not applied for.
Dementia	poor nutrition because client forgets to eat.
History of abusing own children	children are abusive or neglectful of parent.

strengths and limitations and the social, financial, and institutional resources available to the client. The case manager focuses particularly on how these resources are related to the needs of the client—how they are meeting the needs or falling short of maintaining independence. On the basis of this assessment the social worker develops an individualized care plan with the client that identifies priorities, desired outcomes, and the strategies and resources to be used in attaining the outcomes.

In the standard case management system, an individual client is assigned one case manager who either solely manages the case or acts as the leader of a team. It is reasoned that holding one worker responsible for the care given to the client is a strategy for overcoming the neglect and fragmentation that occur when a variety of agencies and providers are not accountable to the others (or, perhaps, not even aware of each other). The more impaired a client, the more likely it is that he or she is receiving services from many sources and the less likely that he or she can manage them alone. Similarly, case managers assigned such clients find that assuming responsibility for service delivery may be the most time consuming but may also highlight the importance of the case manager's role. By designating one person as the case manager, the system is attempting to ensure that there is somebody who is accountable and who is helping the client hold the service delivery system accountable.[8]

The duties of a case manager extend far beyond scheduling services and maintaining organized case records. The competent case manager schedules services to address identified needs in the client's physical and social environment to ease the tension caused by the deterioration of some aspect of the client's condition. The unstable nature of the clients cared for in a case management system requires an insight into the source of difficulties and constant attention to fluctuations in the degrees of seriousness that they take.

This is accomplished by the establishment of a trusting relationship and an accurate assessment of the functioning levels of clients and resources and an ongoing adjustment of services as needed. The case manager must be aware of events that can negatively impact the client's physical and emotional condition, such as death or illness of a relative (or even a pet), eviction, and loss of benefits. Although the emphasis in case management is on linking people with services, case managers in theory do whatever it takes—whether brokerage, advocacy, or resource development—to ensure that all client needs are met; they may even provide a missing service themselves.

CASE EXAMPLE

As part of his supervisory duties, Richard made periodic home visits with the case managers in his agency. Usually this involved accompanying the case managers on their home visits to give him an opportunity to not only interview the clients but also to see the interaction between case managers and their clients.

At ten o'clock one morning, Richard and Nancy were surprised to discover Mrs. Cook still in bed. Her homemaker had not shown up for work, leaving her without assistance in transferring to her wheelchair, getting dressed, or toileting. Mrs. Cook had also depended on the homemaker to prepare a breakfast and therefore had not eaten since early the previous evening.

Rather than immediately phoning the homemaker agency and trying to locate a replacement, Nancy began assisting Mrs. Cook in her personal needs while Richard prepared a full meal for the client. Although Nancy was not trained as a home health aide and therefore only performed the basic tasks for the client's comfort and safety and Richard did not wash the dishes or mop the kitchen afterward, they were able to handle Mrs. Cook's immediate needs until the replacement arrived.

Obviously, dressing clients is not part of a case manager's job description and cooking is certainly not a usual activity of a supervisor. But the client's human needs, and the case management agency's commitment to assist her, took priority.

How Did Case Management Develop?

To understand what case management is, one must first look at the system in which it operates and made it a needed commodity. This system is our society— how it has reacted to the more vulnerable populations and how it has addressed (or not addressed) their needs.

Institutional Bias

Society has operated under an institutional bias regarding the care of the elderly. The first choice has always been to place the frail in hospital or nursing home settings, with consideration of community placement seen only as an alternative. The existence of an institutional bias in the United States appears from the early days of its history. The "poor house" was always overpopulated with the elderly who could not manage to live independently. County homes and state mental hospitals assumed this role by the beginning of the twentieth century, culminating in the 1950s when the state asylums were packed with senile elderly.

Several factors seem to have contributed to this attitude. The evolution of the family unit from an extended, stable group to the nuclear and highly mobile systems we now see has left the elderly living alone, distant from family support. Those caregivers who attempt to care for the elderly at home have seldom had exposure to the frail population and therefore have little prior experience and few role models.

Another principal reason is financial incentives that favor medical service over social services and institutional over noninstitutional care. The services reimbursed by Medicaid and Medicare are mainly care in acute facilities or nursing homes. Therefore, unless sufficient family resources exist, the decision of whether to care for an elder with no assistance or have them institutionalized at no cost amounts to no real decision at all. Over half of nursing home placements are financed by Medicaid.

The fragmentation of the service delivery system is also a contributor to the institutional bias. This characteristic is very easy to identify; simply search the Internet for elderly services. Thousands of providers are offering services from financial planning to anti-aging herbs, and hundreds of in-home care agencies list their services. In any location, an individual might have the choice of many services or none. He or she might be eligible for various payments sources or none. Because these programs are administered by a diverse group of federal, state, and local agencies there is considerable potential for clients to become lost in the system. This results in some clients entering nursing homes because it is the easiest course to take while others remain in the community with inadequate care.

Another factor in this equation is the primary caregiver, often a spouse or sibling, who may also suffer from disabilities that inhibit his or her ability to seek assistance and to pay for in-home care. The primary caregiver may be employed, requiring him or her to choose whether to remain at home without income or leave the disabled family member to care for himself or herself during work hours. The final decision is that of nursing home placement. All of these choices result in stress on the family.

System Pressures

In the past the frail elderly and disabled were cared for either by family members or sent to the "home," as institutional facilities were called. Those elderly without family or requiring more skilled care than could be managed by informal caregivers were sent to nursing homes. Although it might be a distasteful decision, there were few alternatives. Only the wealthy could afford a live-in nurse to care for the frail aged. Four changes in society have affected this pattern.

First, the elderly family member was cared for by the female who also functioned as the housewife, usually a daughter or daughter-in-law who was at home with children while her husband supported the family. The elderly parent was able to move in and receive necessary care. Although the additional responsibility might be burdensome, the wife was expected to accept it as her duty. Economic changes in the last three decades have removed the housewife from those domestic circumstances and placed her in the office. The need for a second income has outweighed the need for child care and elder care.

Second, adult children tended to remain in the vicinity of their elderly parents. Often living in the same town, same neighborhood, or even next door, the need to provide supplemental care to the older family members could be accommodated. Recent changes in the mobility of the population has resulted in a greater distance between families. The pursuit of employment opportunities has moved the younger generation to large cities, often across the country, and many retirees have themselves migrated to the Sunbelt. Both events have left the elderly without close family contact.

Third, following the move to deinstitutionalize the mentally ill came the idea to keep the elderly in the community. This movement may have been prompted by social service professionals but it was quickly adopted by the elderly themselves. As the older population became large, as politicians realized that the elderly are the most reliable voters, and as organizations representing the elderly came into operation, this group began to demand an alternative to institutional care.

Fourth, before Medicaid and Medicare, the nursing home bills were paid by family members or local charities. The county home was the last resort for the indigent. After the two federal programs came into existence, tax monies were used to finance institutional care for a large percentage of placements. The rising cost of care became a significant budget item in the Medicaid budget, both on the state and federal levels. Insurance companies began to feel the pressure of long hospital stays. The need for a cost effective alternative became evident.

Changing Perceptions

Several trends have brought case management into the forefront as an effective method of coordinating care. There has been a change from seeing the clients as persons with physiological and medical abnormalities to a focus on the way the social environment impacts on the individual. This has led to a move away from a medical model, which dictated institutionalization, to the premise that the least restrictive environment is in the client's best interest, or a social–legal model. This has been spurred by the interests in the rights of individuals to determine their own care. It is no longer the authority of a worker to make final judgments on what is best for a client; it has now become accepted for the client to have the final say in what services he or she will receive and where.

The consumer rights movement is not a new phenomenon; it grew out of several complementary social movements that began to emerge in the 1960s and 1970s, including:

- the civil rights movement and legislation
- the development of self-help organizations
- demedicalization and self-care
- deinstitutionalization of the mentally ill population
- the independent living movement of physically disabled people[9]

The History of Case Management

The concept of coordination of services is not new. As early as the 1830s, an inter-denominational group of ministers joined together for mutual aid and consultation in helping the poor. After World War II, services to veterans were offered in a coordinated system in a successful but soon terminated program.

Little was known about case management before the mid-1970s. Its growth as a distinct concept can be linked to the increase in human service programs in the 1960s, which focused on the individual's right to services and resources. Public funding for those service programs was provided largely through categorical channels resulting in a network of services that was highly complex, fragmented, duplicative, and uncoordinated. Programs were designed to treat one distinct problem and to address a small target population because it was easier to pass legislation and funding for limited, tightly restricted groups rather than major programs.[10] Existing governmental functions were expanded incrementally, often adding a population that had little to do with the original focus, creating a jumble of programs with varying eligibility requirements. Therefore, persons with multiple problems, a characteristic of the elderly and disabled, were served by several programs, sometimes working at cross purposes and duplicating efforts while other needs remained unmet. This was particularly true in the gap between health and social service agencies.

As these different programs emerged to offer specialized services or to serve narrowly defined target groups, it was finally realized that the target populations were not being served adequately by disconnected programs dealing with narrow aspects of their problems. It was unrealistic that a client, already suffering from a disability, would be able to locate, apply for, and receive assistance from all programs for which she was eligible.

The Evolution of Coordination of Care

An American Public Welfare Association model in 1971 required that agencies maintain an inventory of specific services to be offered to potential users. A programmer functioned as the agent to channel the user to what was requested. However, it was found that users did not request all the services they needed and most services delivered were those provided by the contacted agency; very few outside resources were utilized.

A demonstration project in Massachusetts for an in-home personal care program for the frail elderly in need of long-term care was not a success because of the overriding bias toward institutionalization. A subsequent program in Connecticut, called Triage, was a success, as were programs in Georgia, Pennsylvania, and Wisconsin. Although exhibiting different approaches, each system used case management as the central vehicle for planning.

There was also a move to deinstitutionalize mental health clients, due mostly to better medication which would allow them to function in the community. But, despite the pharmaceutical assistance, these persons, many of whom had been institutionalized for years, could not cope with the demands made by total independence.

During the early 1970s the Department of Health, Education, and Welfare funded a series of demonstration projects to test various approaches to improving the coordination of federal service programs at the state and local levels. Service integration was designated as a priority by HEW secretary Elliott Richardson. Under the Allied Health Services Act of 1972, forty-five Service Integration Targets for Opportunity demonstration projects were created to improve linkages and coordination at the state and local levels, followed by the Partnership Grants Program in 1974. These projects included two common elements: an expanded variety of community-based services and case management. They focused on the elements needed to coordinate care, featuring such techniques as client tracking, information and referral, interagency pooling and service delivery agreements, one-stop service centers, and specialized management information systems. Most projects also featured case managers called system agents who were expected to coordinate resources for clients and be accountable for their appropriate passage through the service delivery system.[11]

Later legislation focused on specific populations, including the frail elderly, and spurred the development of case management programs as we know them today. The Older Americans Act of 1978 allowed Area Agencies on Aging to provide case management services. In 1981 the Omnibus Budget Reconciliation Act (OBRA) emphasized case management with populations such as the mentally ill, the aged, the developmentally disabled, and children in need of protective services. This bill authorized the secretary of health and human services to issue waivers to section 2176 of the Social Security Act, allowing states to use Medicaid funds to provide a variety of in-home and community-based long-term care services. This included case management to Medicaid-eligible elderly individuals who would otherwise require institutional care. In addition to the 2176 waiver program, many states also began to fund broader community care programs that provided services—including case management—to older people who required assistance with such daily living functions as bathing.[12]

Now that home care had been identified as a cost effective, least restrictive solution, how was it to be administered? As discovered in the mental health experience, simply offering an array of diverse services with varying eligibility requirements was ineffective. There needed to be a single point of application and, more importantly, a single point of responsibility. Physicians and nurses were often asked to arrange medical services and social workers were sought for social services. These two systems from diverse orientations, although having the commonality of the client's welfare, often worked at cross-purposes. The medical team would be scheduling more care while the social worker strived to decrease dependence on the system. Case management has emerged as a response to this fragmentation and is considered to be one step toward improving the long-term care system.

Deinstitutionalization

National policy over the past three decades has sought to minimize the number of people who must rely on institutions for personal assistance. This policy, known as **deinstitutionalization,** has created several important ripple effects. After the discovery of psychotropic drugs in the mid-1950s, mental health systems began moving people from institutional to **community-based care** settings in the belief that the client would benefit from being in the community, which was thought to be more humane.[13] Unfortunately, many deinstitutionalized people with mental illness have encountered a community-based care system lacking in funding and coordination.

Another significant effect is a change in the population that lives in nursing homes. Nursing home residents used to comprise a broad range of persons in various stages of illness and disability. Today nursing homes care primarily for the frailest people, particularly those with significant mental impairments, strokes, or Alzheimer's disease. People in nursing homes tend to have few financial resources and some have no one looking out for their interests. The vulnerability of the deinstitutionalized population has raised concerns about ensuring that their well-being is adequately protected. One person's disability affects many other people. For the many millions of Americans who require help with everyday activities, family and friends are the first line of support. Indeed, one in four Americans currently provides some kind of care for a person who has a chronic condition. In 1990 nearly 83 percent of persons under age 65 with chronic disabilities and 73 percent of disabled persons over 65 relied exclusively on these informal caregivers.[14]

There is general agreement that home care cannot replace institutions in all instances. Particularly for those frail elderly with multiple disabilities or poor housing conditions or who live alone, the usual extent of home care (10–20 hours a week) does not enable them to remain in their homes. At that point the institutional alternative represents the only viable option—and it is probably also the most humane solution even if the quality of life or care in many institutions can be questioned. In addition, with heavily dependent elderly where more than 20–35 hours of home care weekly are necessary the real cost of home care can exceed the costs of institutions. Despite clear differences between home and institutional care, these two possibilities need not inevitably represent an either/or solution. Some institutions provide day care or short stay care in combination with in-home services.[15]

Tasks of Case Managers

Unlike other professions, it is difficult to devise an official list of what a case manager does. Although there is a standardized process which will be discussed at length throughout this text, the actual duties of each case manager varies between peers, with each of their clients, and daily with individual clients. As care is individualized to meet the unique and ever-changing needs of the clients, so too are the tasks the case manager must perform to secure and administer assistance.

One attempt to describe case management activities is a reflection of the mixture of management, sociological, psychological, logical, and humanistic approaches needed:

- developing trust and confidence between worker, agency, and client;
- giving personal understanding to individual client conditions and situations;
- listening to the client sometimes just for the sake of listening because the client wants to talk and because the worker is gathering information for better understanding of the client and the situation;
- leading clients to participate actively in recognizing their own impairments and in restorative activities; mobilizing the client's own network of resources—spouse, family, clubs, church—so that older persons become their own case managers within their individual capacity;
- seeking client preferences and providing information about possible alternatives;
- negotiating conflicts between client preferences, relatives' wishes, and doctor's recommendations;
- offering a professional and experienced opinion regarding plan implementation;
- providing support all along the way through encouraging, reassuring, and approving;
- using reenforcement techniques of rewarding and withholding praise as well as approval for carefully selected aspects of self-care the client has agreed to perform;
- referring for counseling;
- handling barriers and interferences from negative family relationships, other environmental problems, or the client's own anger and hostility;
- finding specialized resources such as for treatment of substance abuse, stroke, and other problems beyond the worker's own capability;
- using a psychological contract approach when appropriate;
- providing some concrete aids for the client: a pill box, night lights, a ramp, a wheelchair;
- educating the client about what the agency does and how it operates.[16]

Any experienced case managers can add various other tasks and roles that they have assumed.

The Evolution Continues

Given the various perspectives on case management, its historical development, and the impact of managed care, it will be necessary to revise the case management process for the future. Shifts are evident in client involvement, the roles of the helper, and the emphasis on cost containment. Historically, the case management process has emphasized coordination of services, interagency cooperation, and advocacy, but the process of service delivery is expanding. Other trends have emerged from federal legislation, including coordination of care, integration of services, and the client as a customer. More recently, professionals providing services have been encouraged to empower clients, contain costs, and assure quality services. These shifts in emphasis are reflected in the roles and responsibilities of the people delivering service today.[17]

E X E R C I S E S

1. Mrs. Patterson calls you, her case manager, to complain that the housing authority has still not repaired the ceiling in her apartment. She tells you that Mr. Whitman, who lives above her, told her that the loose plaster was due to the leak underneath his kitchen sink; he has been trying to get the maintenance man to fix it for several weeks but nothing has been done. Explain what you would do and whether each action is indirect or direct service, macrolevel or microlevel, and horizontal or vertical.

2. Discuss the ways in which the case manager is accountable to the client, the payers, and the providers and how these responsibilities might cause conflict.

3. Russell is a fifteen-year-old quadriplegic, injured in a diving accident. He is physically ready to return home to live with his parents and younger siblings in a middle-class environment. Your initial interview with Russell showed him to be sullen, sarcastic, and (you believe) very scared. In your visit with his parents, you noticed a lack of discipline in the behavior of his seven- and nine-year-old brothers, a three-story home with Russell's room on the top floor, and a room full of football and basketball equipment and trophies. Discuss the environment that Russell will be returning to, how he will affect it, and how the interaction will affect his care.

4. This chapter discusses the changes in society that have led to the need for case management. Discuss how you see the community-based services system changing in the future, considering such factors as a growing elderly population, a reduced birth rate, growth in technology, economic changes, and the political environment.

K E Y T E R M S

case management
payers
client
providers
deinstitutionalization
community-based care

NOTES

1. Austin, C. (1993). Case management: A systems perspective. *Families in Society, 74*(8), 451–459.

2. Roberts-DeGennaro, M. (1987). Developing case management as a practice model. *Social Casework: Journal of Contemporary Social Work, 68*, 466–70.

3. Morrow-Howell, N. (1992). Clinical case management: The hallmark of gerontological social work. *Journal of Gerontological Social Work, 3–4*, 119–31.

4. Rothman, J. (1992). *Guidelines for case management: Putting research to professional use.* Itasca, IL: F. E. Peacock.

5. Roberts-DeGennaro, M. (1987). Developing case management as a practice model. *Social Casework: Journal of Contemporary Social Work, 68*, 466–70.

6. Austin, C. (1993). Case management: A systems perspective. *Families in Society, 74*(8), 451–459.

7. Wolk, J. L., Sullivan, W. P., & Hartmann, D. J. (1994). The managerial nature of case management. *Social Work, 39*(2), 152–160.

8. Rose, S. (1992). *Case management & social work practice.* New York: Longman.

9. Tower, K. D. (1994). Consumer-centered social work practice: Responding client self-determination. *Social Work, 39*(2), 191–196.

10. Dinerman, M. (1992). Managing the maze: Case management and service delivery. *Administration in Social Work, 16*(1), 1–9.

11. Austin, C. (1992). Case management in long term care. In S. M. Rose, (Ed.), *Case management & social work practice.* pp. 199–218. New York: Longman.

12. General Accounting Office. (1993). *Long term care case management: State experiences and implications for federal policy.* GPO.

13. Rubin, A. (1992). Case management. In S. M. Rose, (Ed.), *Case management & social work practice.* pp. 5–20. New York: Longman.

14. General Accounting Office. (1993). *Long term care case management: State experiences and implications for federal policy.* GPO.

15. Topinkova, E. (1994). Care for elders with chronic disease and disability. *Hastings Center Report,* Sept–Oct.

16. Steinberg, R., & Carter, G. (1983). *Case management and the elderly.* Lexington, MA: Lexington Books.

17. Woodside, M., & McClam, T. (1998). *Generalist case management.* Pacific Grove: Brooks/Cole.

2 Case Management Settings

Most of the variations in case management are a result of the types of systems that house the service. *Case management is the* coordination of a specified group of resources and services for a specified group of people. Therefore, except for those practicing private case management, the target population is known, whether it involves a specific location, ailment, age, income, or organizational membership. Often the type of population dictates the way the program is administered, the qualifications of the case managers, and the method of financing.

The specific nature of case management programs varies. One manner of categorizing systems is by identifying the intensity, breadth, and duration of services. *Intensity* refers to the amount of time the case manager has to spend with each client based on caseload size. *Breadth of services* refers to the scope of the clients' problems which will be addressed through a structured and comprehensive assessment and care planning process. *Duration* refers to how long the case manager is involved with the client performing monitoring and reevaluation to adjust care, rather than just collecting data for tracking purposes.[1]

Categorizing by Organization

Case management services differ regarding the context of delivery. Organizational influences include the sponsoring or home agency in which the case management services are offered; the authority of the agency to provide and/or pay for services; the professional group the case management uses as its basis, usually either social work or nursing; and the specific target group for which the case management services are designed.[2] Most case management services are provided by special units within agencies that offer a variety of services. For example, area agencies on aging may establish special case management units to coordinate transportation and nutrition services to the elderly. A corporation, association, or labor union may offer case management to employees or members as a subunit of their human resources department.

One study determined that the organization's primary service, the worker's educational level, and the worker's professional affiliation are the most important variables associated with case management activity. Case managers in home health care performed assessment tasks significantly more frequently than case managers in organizations providing adult day health care or therapy counseling. In addition, case managers in home health care performed care plan implementation activities and advocacy activities significantly less often than workers in the other organizations.[3]

Categorizing by Payment

The source of funding for a program has a major impact on the style and degree of case management. First there are the eligibility requirements, spending caps, and other financial restraints that may be placed on an organization, thereby influencing the qualifications, activities, and caseloads of the case managers. Then the authority to purchase services may rest with the individual case manager or with some other person in the organization or completely outside the agency. As the decision power moves further away from the case manager, the need for persuasion, mutual exchange, negotiations, and sometimes basic pleading is greatly increased.[4]

Some models empower the case managers to authorize funding and to modify or disregard normal eligibility requirements. Other programs establish a cap on spending for each person and require the case manager to maintain costs below the standard. Some systems, such as HMOs, offer little client–case manager interaction but authorize the case manager to approve (or disapprove) of reimbursement for services.[5] The emergence of managed care as a model of health care delivery has increased the demand for case management services and provided new models and definitions of service delivery. Such a role places the case manager as the focus of fiscal management and accountability; when this function assumes primary importance the case manager may become caught between the social/health role and the financial role.[6] To understand its impact, one must first grasp what managed care is.

Managed Care and Case Management

Virtually every American with private health insurance has come into contact with some form of managed care. **Managed care** is a system that, in varying degrees, integrates the financing and delivery of medical care through contracts with selected physicians and hospitals that provide comprehensive health care services to enrolled members for a predetermined monthly premium. All forms of managed care represent attempts to control costs by modifying the behavior of doctors, although they do so in different ways. Most forms also restrict the access of their insured populations to physicians who are not affiliated with a particular plan.

The predominant forms of managed care are:

1. Group and Staff Model Health Maintenance Organizations (HMO)
   a. the most restrictive with fewer choices for the consumer

      b. consumer must choose a primary care physician or one will be assigned

      c. physicians are paid a salary or a set amount per patient (capitation)

  2. Individual Practice Associations (IPAs)

      a. less restrictive form of HMO

      b. individual physicians practice in their own offices under contract

      c. consumer can choose primary care doctor from list of participating physicians

      d. primary care doctor refers to a specialist who belongs to the network

      e. largest number of HMO members are enrolled in the IPA model

  3. Point of Service Plans (POS)

      a. even greater choice and flexibility

      b. use doctors within the network, but have the option to go "out of plan"

      c. "out of plan" visits cost more, most typically in the form of coinsurance and deductibles

  4. Preferred Provider Organizations (PPOs)

      a. networks of doctors and hospitals that have agreed to give discounts on their usual rates

      b. may choose doctors and visit specialists without permission from a gatekeeper

      c. premiums are usually somewhat higher than HMO premiums and there is less coordination of care

By early 1997, one half of the total population was in some type of managed care plan. Seventy-four percent of those receiving their health insurance through their employer, 13 percent of Medicare beneficiaries, and 42 percent of Medicaid beneficiaries were enrolled in a managed care plan.[7] Even traditional fee-for-service health insurance companies have begun integrating elements of managed care into their free-choice health plans to satisfy increasingly cost-conscious customers. As a result, tens of millions of Americans are encountering a growing assortment of cost containment measures—capitation rates, utilization review, coinsurance and copayment fees, deductibles, formularies, gatekeeper physicians, and case managers.

Case management here seeks to increase control of people's behavior in selecting and using health care. By determining what the least costly course of treatment would be, the case manager acts to support the managed care system, then secondarily the managed care client. This goal is reflected within managed care approaches that establish a utilization approach to case management. Access to services that are deemed to be expensive to the system is managed through a gatekeeping function often incorporating prior approval, assessment, or evaluation by a clinical professional.

While the primary goal of cost containment may sound brutal, it should be noted that most clients are interested in services that maximize their independence and place them in the least restrictive environments. For example, a client would rather remain in her home than be placed in a nursing home; in this case, as in most, the least restrictive is also the least costly. So while the motives of the case manager and the client in the managed care system are different, they are not at cross-purposes.

Managed care is also being adopted by the human service delivery system. In these areas, the social service or mental health service delivered has been restricted by the same types of provider agreements as in health plans.[8] The most typical examples of this system are detoxification centers for substance abuse. As managed care plans expand their benefit packages to attract more subscribers, this method of rationing will spread to more types of services. The use of managed care in human services will continue to influence the delivery of services.

Categorizing by Type of Case Manager

Staffing in case management also varies among programs. Some require professionally trained social workers and nurses, others allow more of a case aide model working under the supervision of a professional, and still others utilize volunteers and family members in the role.[9] The worker's educational level and professional affiliation have been found significantly related to case management activity. Case managers with masters degrees perform monitoring tasks significantly less often than case managers with less education. When case management is provided by social workers, advocacy tasks are performed significantly more often than when case management is provided by nurses or other professions.[10]

Primary Care Model

In the primary care model, the physician acts as the case manager. Operating from health maintenance organizations, this is a traditional medical model rather than a social one. Although providing appropriate care in a coordinated fashion is the major goal or primary care case management, controlling the cost of that care is the chief motivation. In an HMO, the physician is paid a set rate per person in the plan (capitation); therefore, he or she is financially at risk for providing excessive care. It becomes the purpose of primary care case management to determine the least costly method of treatment which may lead to under-prescribed services.[11]

The Generalist Case Manager

In a generalist system, one individual has responsibility for being the single source of service contact related to serving a given client. Regardless of the educational background or field, the **generalist** case manager assumes the task of coordinating all professionals and sometimes informal resources, much as a general practitioner does in the field of medicine. With decision making located around one individual, the coordination of care becomes much simpler. The client does not have to deal with an array of different managers from different disciplines, and therefore with varying perspectives on care, and the client as well as the caregivers must only make one contact to report or request changes. From the case manager's point of view, generalist case management usually means a smaller caseload but more intimate knowledge of each client and their specific characteristics, seen as providing more accurate and personal care.

Unfortunately, there is sometimes the implication that a generalist is a "jack of all trades, master of none" while a specialist is expert in one particular area and therefore more professional. Heus and Pincus[12] describe the creative generalist as an expert in problem solving, networking, and coalition building to find unique, responsive solutions. The ability to see the whole picture of clients and their environment and to make appropriate changes so they function more effectively is the skill of the generalist. Locke et al.[13] list generalist qualities as the ability to work with a variety of issues of concern, to work with diverse client systems, to influence change at multiple levels, and to apply intervention strategies that address multiple problems. In other words, the generalist case manager *can* see the forest and not just the trees.

One disadvantage of this approach is that the generalist case manager is expected to have a wide range of skills and knowledge, which may have cost implications. Another is the emotional burden taking full responsibility for a client may create, especially when dealing with a long-term care population characterized by multiple, chronic, and often unsolvable problems.

The Specialist Case Manager

In a **specialist** case management system, a client is assigned several different case managers, depending on the needs and services reflected by the assessment. Often representing different disciplines or areas of expertise, a team structure is formed and each player addresses those issues within their field. Normally, regularly scheduled conferences, both with and without the presence of the client, allow the team members to discuss the plan of care and assure its acceptance by all. This structure offers the clients a higher degree of skill and allows the case managers to develop this level by focusing on a narrower subject than a generalist must deal with. The sharing of responsibility reduces the chance of burnout or feelings of isolation.

A major disadvantage to the specialist method is the determination of jurisdiction. While the professionals may have difficulty on occasion deciding how to assign responsibility within the group, the client and caregiver may have great confusion deciding which case manager is appropriate for which issue. The outside agencies providing services may also experience frustration when trying to select which specialist is appropriate in each situation. By sharing responsibility, the danger of duplicated, overlapping, contrary, or neglected services is increased, particularly when one or more members of the team do not cooperate fully.

Case managers may specialize based on the functions they perform or the type of caseload they carry. An intake case manager, perhaps a masters level social worker or nurse, assesses the client's needs and develops the care plan. Then an ongoing case manager, usually with bachelor level training, assumes responsibility for implementing the care plan once a client's immediate needs are met. Case managers may also develop expertise in working with specific types of cases such as spinal injury or Alzheimer's. Specialized case managers may have smaller caseloads because their work tends to involve short-term crisis oriented situations that demand constant attention,[14] for example, ventilator-dependent children.

A modified use of the specialist models uses nurses and social workers as teams. The team may conduct the initial assessment and develop the care plan, but the task of monitoring falls to one member. When changes arise in the client's condition, consultation with the team is expected. Although designed so that the most appropriate case manager would be assigned for an individual client, the higher salary of nurses has forced many organizations to utilize them only in the assessment phase and consistently use social workers as ongoing monitors.

The Specialist–Generalist Model

In this approach the client is assigned a single case manager who performs multiple tasks as in the generalist model. In some cases, the specialist–generalist is trained in a particular discipline, such as psychotherapy, and is expected to perform these specialized skills as well as the generalist tasks. While ensuring that the case manager, as the only contact for the client, maintains total knowledge of the client, it has the disadvantage of restricting the field to only those case managers with specialized training. It may also lead the case manager to focus on the area of specialization while, either from lack of knowledge or lack of interest, ignoring other needs of the client.[15]

It can be argued that a generalist will become a specialist in a variety of areas: a case manager at an area agency on aging will specialize in the elderly clients, adult children as caregivers, the region the agency covers, home care rather than institutional care. A case manager for a juvenile probation office will specialize in teenage problems, substance abuse, gang behavior, the justice system, and the public education system. What differentiates this model from the generalist model is that the speciality involved is the central focus of the client/case manager relationship.

The Therapist–Case Manager

A variation on this theme is the proposal that case managers are really all therapists —that the required in-depth knowledge of a client's characteristics and everyday life are needed to accurately assess strengths and weaknesses and to respond to them. While the length or depth of the relationship may be restricted (more than likely by caseload size), the overriding purpose of a case manager is to assist clients in resolving problems, which is defined as therapy. Rather than attempting adjustments to the thought processes of the client, the therapist–case manager attempts to adjust the social environment.[16]

Categorizing by Case Manager Function

Various studies have identified three models of case management—a broker model, a service management model, and a managed care model.

The Brokerage Model

The case manager as a **broker,** or arranger of services, is a common type of arrangement. The goal of case management is frequently to reduce institutional care among clients at risk of nursing home admission through access to available community-based long-term care. In this model, the case manager acts to overcome the lack of information, uncoordinated services, and distorted financial incentives in the long-term care system.

In this model, public or private nonprofit organizations provide case management services, with either little or no authority to purchase services for the clients or by serving clients eligible to receive community-based long-term care under Medicaid, Medicaid waivers, or some other publicly funded program, such as a state program, an Older Americans Act program, or one using pooled funds. The case management agency serves a coordinating function and may also be a service provider.

There may be a cap on what can be spent per month per client on community-based long-term care. Case managers can only arrange community-based long-term care that is already available through existing programs. Outreach may be minimal and screening or even assessment may be done by another group such as a preadmission screening program. The budget, the program caseload, or the caseload per worker may be fixed, often causing programs to have waiting lists.[17]

Disagreements arise on the level of professionalism called for when the case manager is responsible for arranging care without personally providing any care. One side states that brokerage models are simplistic, do not call for professional judgement, and are merely bureaucratic arrangements to facilitate service delivery. The other camp argues that training and professional skills are required for accurate assessments, care plans, and monitoring. They point out that the complex lives of typical case managed clients cannot be organized by a paraprofessional, that the varied psychological and physical manifestations observed by case managers must be translated into services needed or referred for specific attention. Also, the broker must be sensitive to the wishes, as well as the needs, of the client and possess the professional training to determine a blend between the two.[18]

The Service Management Model

Case managers who view themselves as managers with the primary charge of getting work done through others will attain a broader perspective on their responsibilities. In some ways, a case manager operating under this model will operate as

TABLE 2.1   Comparison of Management and Case Management Tasks

Interpersonal Roles	Management	Case Management
	figurehead	representing agency at function
	leader	motivate clients, provide training
	liaison	create contacts for goal attainment
Informational	monitor	collecting information
	disseminator	providing information to client on services, to service providers on client needs
	spokesperson	provide information on agency to client or other agencies
Decision making	entrepreneur	creating networks between clients and opportunities
	disturbance handler	addressing conflicts between clients, family, providers
	resource allocator	determining amount, type, and cost of services
	negotiator	participating in consultations, policy decisions

Wolk, J. L., Sullivan, W. P., & Hartmann, D. J. (1994). The managerial nature of case management. *Social Work, 39* (2), 152–159.

the manager of a small business—dealing with suppliers, customers, and the general public in order to operate efficiently yet effectively. Table 2.1 illustrates the similarities between the activities a manager of any business performs and the activities the case manager often enacts.

In both cases there are organizational, interpersonal, and public roles to fill; each must not only create a balance of the functions but is expected to bounce back and forth among diverse activities as the situation demands. This chart also illustrates the other dimensions of case management: client versus caseload; focused, long-term relationship versus short time need; and dealing with a package of services as well as individual ones.

The Managed Care Model

In capitated programs, the case management organization is at risk for all long-term care services specified under the managed care plan whether provided directly or not. Because the HMO's profit depends on keeping the costs of acute care down, the incentive for appropriate case finding and management is increased.

The goal of the case management unit is to minimize total costs for its organization. Paid an annual amount from Medicare or Medicaid, the case managers are expected to allocate services to enrollees so funds spent on community-based services prevent the higher costs of acute care.

Case Management with Society as the Client

There has been an increase in approaches and models of case management designed to administer social control rather than social support. These programs focus on the protection of the community rather than the protection of the individuals receiving its services. Whether the goal is to make dependency less expensive or to reduce disorder and disruption of the community by the population, controlling behavior (whether overt or just financially burdensome) becomes the goal.[19]

The entry of case management into the criminal justice field has added a new dimension to the role. Positions formerly labeled as parole officers are sometimes either given tasks like those of the traditional case manager (service coordination, linkage, and brokering) or actually given the title of case manager. Seen as less expensive than incarceration, the maintenance of offenders in the community while monitoring their activities, sometimes with electronic equipment, has become a popular trend. Critics, however, charge that these functions create an ambiguity as to whether the client or society is truly the receiver of benefits.

Similar questions arise when the clientele are those who have received mental commitments and are being allowed to remain in the community under surveillance. In these cases, the case manager is interested in meeting the needs of the clients while still coercing them to behave in a socially nondisruptive manner.[20]

The state of Washington utilizes case managers placed in nursing homes to identify the residents who have the potential for moving into the community and to develop plans of care for their discharge.[21]

The result of these various dimensions is the lack of a standardized model of a case management system. This has significant implications on research, whether the subject is cost effectiveness, case management tasks, or client outcomes.

EXERCISES

1. You are the case manager for Karen, a cancer patient. Karen is a single mother with two preschool children, limited income from a disability pension and occasional assistance from her sister, who has her own family. Discuss how your approach would vary using the following case management methods: the brokerage model, the service management model, and the managed care model.

2. You have been asked to design a new case management service for the homeless. Your first decision is to decide whether you need generalists, specialists, specialist–generalists, or therapists. Discuss which type (or combination) you would select and the advantages and disadvantages of your decision.

3. A criticism of case management systems is that they downplay the "management" role. Discuss how using management techniques in everyday case management could both positively and negatively affect service delivery.

4. Rachel is a fourteen-year-old girl with a long history of disruptive behavior and encounters with the legal system. The court has sent her to a halfway house for delinquents where her every move is monitored and Rachel is pleading with you to return home, promising that she will attend school regularly, disassociate herself from the street gang, and stop shoplifting. Discuss the elements of client self-determination and the protection of society, how these two clash in Rachel's case, and what you would do.

KEY TERMS

managed care
generalist
specialist
broker

NOTES

1. Austin, C. (1993). Case management: A systems perspective. *Family in Society, 74*(8), 451–459.
2. Douville, M. L. (1993). Case management: Predicting activity patterns. *Journal of Gerontological Social Work, 20* (3/4), 43–55.
3. Ibid.
4. Rothman, J. (1992). *Guidelines for case management: Putting research to professional use.* Itasca, IL: F. E. Peacock.
5. Morrow-Howell, N. (1992). Clinical case management: The hallmark of gerontological social work. *Journal of Gerontological Social Work, 183* (3–4), 119–31.
6. Austin, C. (1993). Case management: A systems perspective. *Families in Society, 74*(8), 451–459.
7. American Association of Retired Persons. (1997). Managed care: A consumer's guide. AARP WebPlace, www.aarp.org.
8. Woodside, M., & McClam, T. (1998). *Generalist case management.* Pacific Grove: Brooks/Cole.
9. Morrow-Howell, N. (1992). Clinical case management: The hallmark of gerontological social work. *Journal of Gerontological Social Work, 3–4,* 119–31.
10. Douville, M. L. (1993). Case management: Predicting activity patterns. *Journal of Gerontological Social Work, 20* (3/4): 43–55.
11. Rothman, J. (1992). *Guidelines for case management: Putting research to professional use.* Itasca, IL: F. E. Peacock.
12. Heus, M., & Pincus, A. (1986). *The creative generalist: A guide to social work practice.* Barneveld, WI: Micamar Publishing.
13. Locke, B., Garrison, R., & Winship, J. (1998). *Generalist social work practice: Context, story and partnerships.* Pacific Grove, CA: Brooks/Cole.
14. General Accounting Office. (1993). *Long term care case management: State experiences and implications for federal policy.* Washington, DC: GPO.

15. Rothman, J. (1992). *Guidelines for case management: Putting research to professional use.* Itasca, IL: F. E. Peacock.

16. Roberts-DeGennaro, M. (1987). Developing case management as a practice model. *Social Casework: Journal of Contemporary Social Work, 68,* 466–70.

17. Davidson, G. B., Penrod, J. (1991). Modeling the costs of case management in long-term care. *Health Care Financing Review, 13* (1), 73–82.

18. Morrow-Howell, N. (1992). Clinical case management: The hallmark of gerontological social work. *Journal of Gerontological Social Work, 3–4,* 119–31.

19. Moxely, D. P. (1997). *Case management by design.* Chicago: Nelson-Hall.

20. Ibid.

21. Fralich, J., Riley, T., Mollica, R., et al. (1995). *Reducing the cost of institutional care: Downsizing, diversion, closing and conversion of nursing homes.* Portland, ME: National Academy of State Health Policy.

3 The Processes of Case Management

A case management system, in its capacity as a "system," has a prescribed procedure to follow to accomplish the goals of the program. Whether in the fields of mental health, health care, social rehabilitation, criminal justice, or aging, case managers typically perform a common set of sequential and often overlapping functions. The basic phases of client activity can be labeled as follows:

Outreach	Process of creating an awareness in the professional community and in the general public of the availability of services in order to identify and establish contact with those who are appropriate for case management services.
Referral	Process through which various persons in the community in need of case management are referred to the program.
Prescreening	Process through which the client's need for case management is evaluated.
Assessment	Process by which the health, functional, social, psychological, cognitive, financial, environmental, and support needs of a client are identified utilizing a structured assessment instrument.
Care Planning	Process of developing goals to meet client's needs and identification of services necessary to achieve those goals.
Monitoring	Process through which the case manager maintains contact on a regular basis with the client, the client's family, and the providers of service in order to ensure that the services are appropriate and meeting the individual client's current needs.
Reassessment	Process whereby client status, function, and outcomes are reviewed according to an established time frame.
Disengagement	Process of gradual or sudden withdrawal of services, as the situation indicates, on a planned basis.

Although each of these functions is likely to be performed by case managers at some point with each client, there may be a wide degree of latitude about how these tasks are implemented, and even in whether a single case manager provides all these functions. Case managers may also have direct service roles, such as client and caregiver training in the use of assistive aids or equipment, or in how to access other community resources. It should be understood that such categories are not mutually exclusive and that an activity that a case manager performs, such as a home visit, can encompass more than one purpose. It is also common for several activities to occur to address a single purpose.

Sometimes an emergency or crisis situation may shorten or omit a step or rearrange the sequence of events. Agencies with a waiting list or a funding shortage may only be able to offer referrals to those seeking assistance.

Outreach, Referral, and Prescreening

Outreach

The process of creating an awareness in the professional community and in the general public of the availability of services in order to identify and establish contact with those who are appropriate for case management services is called **outreach.**

Potential clients will either be looking for assistance or will have been mandated to receive it. The latter category will have been referred by a system of criminal justice, welfare, or mental health. For an agency that deals exclusively with assigned cases, outreach is not an issue. If, however, a program is attempting to reach a vulnerable population which probably has never heard the term "case management," much less knows how to go about locating an agency that provides it, then outreach becomes critical for two reasons.

First, the agency needs to stay in business—no clients, no income. Even in a large organization in which case management is a small unit, which is usually the case, there must be some activity to justify its existence. Second, a service is being offered that is believed to benefit persons in need, and to be able to assist them you have to locate them.

The emphasis on the outreach functions performed by a case manager is directly related to the agency's capacity to accept new clients. In an infant program, outreach can be the primary function in the beginning in order to build a caseload. As restrictive elements come into play, such as limited funding, full caseloads, or time-limited projects, the performance of outreach activities will, by necessity, lessen or cease.

Because most case management systems are targeted toward a specific population, effective outreach should first identify the characteristics of that population, distinguish one or more common contacts of that population and further identify the persons with the authority to make referrals. The stricter the criteria for admission into the program, the more precise the search for clients should be. Failure to properly structure an outreach program will result in service requests from those inappropriate for assistance while missing those for whom services were originally designed.

How People Find Services.   Too often, locating assistance is a hit or miss operation. Many persons needing case management, such as the elderly, have never applied for health or social services before and are unaware of how to locate help. It is not uncommon for someone to call an agency but not know what type of assistance they need. For example, a man might call requesting a nurse to assist his mother. When asked what type of help his mother needs, he explains that she cannot get in and out of a bathtub alone. Obviously, a nurse is an inappropriate and expensive provider of personal care. With such lack of knowledge, the ordinary consumer will call several agencies listed in the telephone book and select the one that sounded the most promising. While several states have instituted single entry systems for long-term care, in which every applicant for any long-term care service goes through an assessment process to determine what is most appropriate, even these states do not offer the same service for all populations, such as the homeless. And in most locations, the potential clients or their caregivers are on their own.

Once a system is in operation, current or former recipients become an active outreach. Many clients will tell the case manager about a relative or neighbor who is in need of services. One lady who lived in an elderly housing project advertised her case manager's services so widely that the case manager was greeted by a group meeting during a regular visit. The client had organized a surprise party to help the case manager "get more work." Apparently she thought the case manager was paid on a per capita basis; this was her means of thanking the case manager for her assistance.

How Services Find People.   Determining other services or agencies that your target population might utilize serves as an excellent place to start in recruiting clients. Table 3.1 illustrates the variety of referral sources; each community will contain additional resources to be utilized. Each referral should be followed by of notification of whether the case was accepted for services.

It should be noted that the very persons and agencies that can be used for outreach can also serve as service resources for active clients. A rehabilitation worker who can use the case management system as a supplemental resource for clients will be more agreeable to supplying services to referrals from the case management agency. This rather symbiotic relationship advances the care available for everyone's clients and creates an effective network in the community.

One disadvantage in using only professional sources of referral to reach those who most need services, those who are without any form of assistance, is that these persons have not yet been identified by an agency. Therefore, it is necessary to use other means, either reaching potential clients directly or soliciting the involvement of agencies not usually connected with social services.

For this reason, a number of governmental and nongovernmental organizations have adopted street outreach as a core program activity to provide services to underserved or hard-to-reach persons. *Street outreach* is defined as going out of

TABLE 3.1   Referral Sources for Various Populations

Target Population	Referral Sources
Rural Elderly	Title III Meal Sites
	Clinics
	Churches
Homeless	Homeless Shelters
	Police Department
Low Income	Welfare Office
	Food Stamp Office
	Social Security Office
	Unemployment Office
Disabled	Hospital Discharge Planners
	Physicians
	Rehabilitation Agencies

the traditional agency setting and seeking the target populations where they live, congregate, work, patronize, or otherwise independently access goods and services. Persons representing members of the target communities (such as former gang members, battered women, or IV drug users) may be utilized to perform outreach services because of their knowledge of and acceptance by clients.[1] Social workers in a rehabilitation hospital established an outreach service for recent amputees using volunteers with previous amputations. The amputees acted as role models, offering emotional support and information.[2]

Outreach can also be accomplished by publicity to the general public. Presentations to civic and church groups and posters in the senior centers and at the community store will lead to inquiries. For example, a program seeking women who had not received prenatal care organized a series of health fairs in low-income areas to identify women who were pregnant and needed prenatal care. Attendance and participation was enhanced by the contribution of prizes and free items by local businesses. From the registration forms, a list for follow-up contacts was constructed.[3]

Businesses that deal with the public, such as banks, utilities, and pharmacies, may be aware of persons unable to handle their own affairs because of disabilities. Although these will likely lead to fewer "good" referrals since there is no element of screening involved, it is still an important part of outreach.

Referral

Referral is the process through which various persons in the community in need of case management are referred to the program. Each agency, and sometimes each case manager, has a referral source that is more active and more reliable than others. For some, medically based programs such as hospital discharge planners, home health agencies, or physicians contribute the bulk of referrals. Others rely on socially based referrals such as social service agencies, senior centers, aging programs, or churches. There is also a good number of referrals that come through the community by knowledge of a client presently receiving services. These contacts will usually be from the client or the client's family.

Hot lines, a popular method of crisis intervention, may also serve as a useful source of referrals. Publicized in the media, or through individual encounters with friends, family members, a telephone operator, the police, an agency, or former hot line callers, these telephone systems often attract those persons who are unsure of where to obtain help. Specialized crisis lines may address a host of health, legal, financial, and social issues: assault and rape, elder care, cocaine abuse, learning disabilities, alcohol, suicide, parenting, child abuse, and eating disorders.[4]

A referral should offer the necessary demographic information to allow an interview to be scheduled as well as give the case manager the interested person's perception of the presenting problem. It is also helpful to know if the client is aware of the referral.

Prescreening

Prescreening is the process through which the person's need for case management is evaluated. An organized screening of applicants strengthens a program's capability to reach the client population that is most at risk. By using professional judgement, the case manager must distinguish between those in need and those at risk.

Effective prescreening allows case managers to utilize their time and resources on cases with a greater possibility of approval, rather than on functioning as a referral point. It is also to the benefit of those applying for services to be appropriately referred; the elderly and disabled do not need the irritation of hoping for services, going through an involved assessment process only to be told that services are not available to them.

This evaluation looks at the person's eligibility for the program, willingness to participate, most urgent needs (for emergency assistance or referral), and ability to benefit from the program. As with the outreach process, the more specific the eligibility criteria for a program are, the more detailed the prescreening process should be. New programs, in their efforts to become operational, will often have broader requirements than those with waiting lists.

It has become common for professional referrals sources, once they have become familiar with a program, to perform a prescreening activity of their own, so that when a client is referred to the case management agency, the case manager can reasonably conclude that the client is eligible and appropriate for services. Some systems will develop a prescreening document to be used by not only the case manager but also to be distributed to the referral sources.

For the articulate client or caregiver, the prescreening can be accomplished over the telephone. However, if the case manager doubts the validity of the answers received, a home visit is appropriate.

Another function of prescreening is to make the client aware of the program, its benefits, and its limitations. The client or family may be misinformed as to what types or what amounts of services can be given. The responsibilities of the family in the provision of care need to be carefully outlined at the beginning, as well as the reasons care might be terminated. It is wise to furnish such policy in written form to avoid future problems.

EXERCISES

1. You have been asked to speak before the Kiwanis Club to explain what case management is and what services your agency offers. What points will you cover?

2. Your client needs more services than your agency allows. You feel that the limits are arbitrary and that the client should receive the additional assistance. What do you do?

3. In the process of assessing a client, you realize that the client could benefit from mental health services. How do you approach the client and his family?

4. You have discovered that a discharge planner at a local hospital is a convenient source of referrals. What dangers lie in this arrangement?

5. You are making your initial contact with a potential client who was referred by her niece. Introduce yourself.

6. The client tells you that he's gotten along without the government interfering in his life so far and he doesn't need it now. Your observation of the situation tells you services are critical. How do you convince him to accept help?

KEYWORDS

outreach
referral
prescreening

NOTES

1. Valentine, J., & Aguero, L. (1996). Defining the components of street outreach for HIV prevention: The contact and the encounter. *Public Health Reports, 111* (1), 68–74.
2. Wells, L. M., & Schachter, B. (1993). Enhancing rehabilitation through mutual aid: Outreach to people with recent amputations. *Health & Social Work, 18* (3), 221–229.
3. Walrop, D., & Taylor, N. D. (1994). A community hospital's role in lowering infant rates through a maternal access-to-care program. *Health & Social Work, 19* (2), 148–153.
4. Loring, M. T., & Wimberly, E. T. (1993). The time-limited hot line. *Social Work, 38* (3), 344–347.

CHAPTER

4 Assessment

Assessment is the process by which the health, functional, social, psychological, cognitive, financial, environmental, and support needs of a client are identified utilizing a structured assessment instrument.

The Purpose of the Assessment

The job of the case manager is to determine what the client needs but does not have and what demands are made on him that he lacks the capacity to meet—this is the purpose of the assessment. Having made this determination, the case manager can begin to plan how to meet the needs and modify the demands or increase the capacities for meeting them. Specifically, the case manager conducts the following activities:

1. Appraise existing conditions, both the client's personal characteristics and environmental characteristics.
2. Identify gaps in existing conditions that make the client vulnerable.
3. It is then appropriate to identify the uniqueness of the individual and the surrounding influences.

The assessment is the constant element in case management programs. It is also the central element; it clarifies program eligibility and identifies strengths as well as weaknesses through a systematic evaluation of the client's current level of functioning in ever-increasing detail and accuracy.[1] It provides an extended conversational exchange of information to allow observation of the client's behavioral and cognitive characteristics and provides the foundation for the case manager/client relationship. It becomes the basis of decisions on the scheduling of care and assessing the outcomes. Although the activity of assessment is usually connected with the initial evaluation of the client, it is important to realize that the process of assessment is ongoing throughout the life of the case.

The Assessment Document

While assessment documents vary from program to program, most have these common elements:

1. An assessment of health status, identifying disease, injury, and functional ability
2. An assessment of the elements in the client's life that affect their living and/or working environment
3. An assessment of the informal support system, such as family, neighbors, and friends, who provide either tangible or emotional support
4. An assessment of how these factors interact with one another[2]

The assessment process is more than filling in blank spaces on a questionnaire; it is also the mental process of the case manager in judging how the physical, environmental, behavioral, psychological, economic, and social factors interact with each other. It is important to remember that an assessment not only appraises the weaknesses of the client and the client's support system, but that the strengths of the situation are also recognized and used as supplements to the care plan. To obtain the most complete information, one must go beyond the client's contribution and obtain the input of relevant specialists. All professionals involved in the client's care should contribute to the assessment.

Family members, particularly those who have held the role of primary caregiver, are a major source of information on the needs of their relatives. Whereas formal caregivers or providers may report on the current state of functioning, families can better describe the history of illness and treatment. They are also in the best position to recognize the early signs of deterioration and relapse and, particularly those sharing a home with the client, can provide accurate information on sleeping or eating schedules, substance abuse, or memory loss that the client is unwilling or unable to disclose.[3]

Interviewing for an Assessment

The information on the assessment is only as valid as the source of the information. Therefore, taking steps to increase accurate responses will produce better results as the case progresses. An **interview** is, after all, a form of communication in which information is exchanged. The case manager may be sharing information about the agency and its services while the applicant may be describing the problem. They are both also contributing attitudes, values, and expectations. These initial exchanges are the formation of the case manager/client relationship and will influence future activities.

Disrupting the routine, especially of a client with orientation problems, can result in hostility or confusion. When scheduling the home visit with the client, the case manager should determine first what schedule the client may be following to avoid arriving during meal time, nap time, or visits by formal or informal service providers. It is also not necessary that a complete assessment be accomplished in one sitting; a return visit may be scheduled if the client becomes tired or confused.

Case managers need to be cautious about the impression they give while performing the assessment—an impression that each item questioned is an item that can be solved. On the one hand, the case manager needs to know what the client wants, what type of life they want to live, and what needs they have in order to reach their goals. On the other hand, the discussion of these issues can often lead the client to believe that the case manager or the agency is capable of accomplishing the goals, which may lead to disappointment when they fail to produce. Table 4.1 illustrates some possible misconceptions derived from ordinary assessment questions.[4] Arguably, every statement a case manager makes can be misinterpreted and this problem should in no way prevent or curtail open discussion with clients. It is, however, a possible outcome which, if identified at the beginning, will assist the case manager in identifying and addressing unrealistic expectations.

Case management assessments attempt to balance medical and psychosocial components, an effort that requires going beyond the objective questions on the assessment forms. The case manager may ask about available family members but must determine if these are stable and beneficial relationships or if they are detrimental to the client. The client may live alone; this may be sign of isolation and rejection or it could represent liberation to the client. When asking what other services the client receives, the case manager should go past their existence and discover their attitude toward the services and their evaluation of the impact they have on the client's independence.

Case managers can also contribute to the collection of misinformation. Sometimes after interviewing many clients the case manager will become insensitive to differences and begin a stereotyping process. They may fail to pursue a subject because they assume they know the answer, or because they have never found it useful with other clients. Still others will hesitate to ask about subjects they consider unpleasant or embarrassing, such as alcohol use, sexual habits, or death.

TABLE 4.1   Misinterpretations of Assessment Questions

The Case Manager Asks	The Client Says	The Client Thinks
Can you still drive?	Yes, but only if my car gets the transmission fixed.	Maybe they will fix the transmission.
What type of job are you looking for?	I know how to type and file.	The case manager is going to find me a job.
Is this house big enough for all of you?	Not really, we could use a bigger place.	The case manager is going to arrange for new housing.

Other factors may intervene to cause a gap in comprehension. Cultural or age differences between the case manager and the client can introduce different vocabularies or syntaxes that leave the case manager bewildered. Particularly with a teenage population, words may carry a totally different meaning.

One method of easing into the assessment is by moving from external to internal. That is, start with problems in the environment and move to the client's internal functioning—from problems with shopping to problems with sleeping.

Interviewing the Elderly

Validity of responses is a major issue that must be addressed when interviewing the frail elderly. Due to varying disabilities and limits of the people being assessed, it is generally impossible for interviewers to ask the same question in the same manner for all assessments. Although all questions should be asked in a generally consistent manner, the frail and elderly have numerous points of reference, agendas, and levels of comprehension. An interviewer must also be concerned with the level of mental ability; although confused clients may have information to give, they may not make accurate statements.

It is believed that elderly clients do not give information as accurately during their first contact with an agency as they do in subsequent interviews.[5] This underscores the need for the case manager to constantly evaluate the client at each encounter to verify the accuracy of the information on which care is based.

Determining Competency

A referral may neglect to inform the case manager that the client is not mentally or physically capable of providing accurate information. Even when there have been advance reports of senility, incompetence, or depression, the case manager begins with the client as the primary source of information, then turns for supplementary information to family and friends as needed, with the permission of the client. The case manager should also determine if the client has a legal guardian or conservator before making any suggestions to the client. Additional information can be obtained from a doctor, agency case records, other agencies, or neighbors, whatever is appropriate. Beginning with the client is important not only for obtaining relevant data but also for communicating to all concerned that the client has basic rights of privacy and self-determination regardless of being elderly or disabled.

The Interview Setting

Where does the interview take place? Interviews generally take place in an office at agencies, schools, hospitals, and other institutions. Sometimes, however, they are held in an applicant's home. In such cases, the case manager has the distinct advantage of observing the applicant in the home, which gives information about the applicant that may not be available in an office setting.

The Assessment Content

Demographic Information

Demographic information includes items that identify the person and their surroundings. Items will include such things as name, address, telephone numbers, age, gender, marital status, and residence information. The section of the assessment that deals with demographic information, while providing the basis for the case record, also identifies several potential issues.

The location and type of housing and the number of persons in the residence provide a beginning for understanding the client's lifestyle. The location of the client residence may prove to be in a problematic area or neighborhood. The identification of problems or potential problems created from the client's environment is a significant benefit of conducting the interview in the home. Observation used in conjunction with a standardized assessment tool can lead to a more accurate representation of the facts in a case.

Assessing Relationships

The relationship of the persons in the household, as well as the client's satisfaction with the arrangements must be determined. Dysfunctional relationships with family members may indicate a variety of problems such as mental illness, unresolved psychological conflicts, long-standing resentments, or the client's fear of losing autonomy. There is also the possibility of detecting a case of child abuse or elder abuse or neglect.

For younger clients, especially teenaged ones, the key to family relationships may be within the sibling structure. Often an older brother or sister has served as a role model, whether positive or negative, and little progress can be made until that relationship is identified. The peer network also comes into play more with this population, sometimes exerting more behavioral influence than the family.

Development of a comprehensive understanding of the client's relationships with friends, family members, spouse, and other unrelated people is a major portion of the assessment. This understanding will allow the case manager to determine the client's strengths, weaknesses, and coping mechanisms. It will also help to determine the care plan by building on informal supports and individual strengths.

Assessing Informal Resources

The assessment should also contain a section that identifies support systems. The elderly or disabled client is asked if they feel that they need help in performing the activities of daily living and if someone is available to provide that help. The pregnant teenager is asked if she has prenatal care and a source of emotional support. The type of relationship (such as a neighbor versus a family member) gives an indication of the type of task that can be expected (shopping versus bathing assistance).[6]

If the client perceives a need and states that they currently have assistance, it should be determined whether that person or agency has helped them in the past. It is not uncommon for a frail client to state that they have several helping persons who later deny a willingness to assist the client. This misstatement may be due to client error, caregiver burnout, or fear of nursing home placement by the client. Other clients may deny that they need help because they see it as admitting they are not tough enough to handle their own problems, or they have an unwillingness to appear needy.

Informal supports can offer more than material goods or discrete acts of service. A client may depend on a network of family and friends for emotional support, for companionship, or for a connection to the outside world. Specific aspects of social support, such as having a spouse or adult child caregiver or having a caregiving relationship of at least three years' duration, lessen the risk of entering a nursing home.[7] Case managers will have clients whose spouses experience disabilities to the same degree as the client, or even worse. While these caregivers may not be able to handle physical tasks around the home or assist the client in personal care, the emotional caring they provide is almost tangible and is arguably more important to the health of the client than any duty of a home health aide.

The complexities of informal relationships may make the assessment process seem overwhelming and lure those in the health and social services into unquestioningly perceiving families as resources for clients, a desirable alternative to institutionalization. Experience, however, points out that families are not always a suitable care system and, in fact, may be a source of poor care, neglect, or even abuse.

Assessing the Primary Caregiver

A very important segment of the assessment for elderly and disabled clients focuses on the **primary caregiver**. The role of the caregiver is a very complex one and it is no easy process to determine which individuals will fill this role successfully. There is no magic method for assessing caregivers, only an understanding that some information is easily accessible on initial evaluation while other information comes with clinical judgement and skill through repeated contacts over a period of time.

Who Is the Caregiver?   The client may receive care from an entire network of family members, but generally the case manager is interested in identifying the one who assumes responsibility, if not for direct care, at least for coordinating care. This is not always clear, for example, when the designated caregiver is also of an advanced age and experiencing severe physical health problems. Therefore, in identifying the primary caregiver, one must focus on the caregiver's age, health condition, and functional status. The caregiver may be willing and well motivated, but because of other demands may be performing poorly. The location of the caregiver is also important. Do they live with the client, across town, or in another state?

It is not enough to know that the caregiver is a spouse, child, or sibling. One must explore the relationship between the caregiver and the client in the past because past patterns may affect current interactions. The person thrust into caring for a person with whom they have a history of conflict is likely to experience even more anger and guilt than usual. One caregiver whose responsibilities included bathing, dressing, and feeding his confused mother admitted that he had left home as a teenager because he despised his mother.

How Did They Get the Job?   An equally important and related issue is how the caregiver role was established. In the preceding scenario, the man became the caregiver out of default as no one else was willing or able to do so, but he made it clear that he felt an obligation rather than a desire. Adult children are more likely to provide care to a parent of the same gender and infirm elders are more likely to receive care from a child of the same gender. Daughters are a traditional source of assistance in the care of their elderly parents. They were 3.22 times more likely than sons to provide assistance with Activities of Daily Living (ADLs), such as bathing, dressing, and toileting, and 2.56 times more likely to provide assistance with Instrumental Activities of Daily Living (IADLs), such as cooking, cleaning, and shopping.[8] Because the substantial majority of elderly parents requiring care from children are women, this tendency toward gender consistency in the caregiving relationship partially accounts for the fact that daughters are more likely than sons to be involved in parent care.[9]

A large proportion of caregivers work outside of the home. Gorey, Rice, and Brice[10] report that approximately one fifth to one quarter of employees provide care for an elderly dependent. Whether they would be able to do so without supportive services, or whether the 57.3 percent who are not so employed would be if not for caregiving responsibilities is a popular topic in policy discussions. It is proposed that physical and psychological involvement in elder care predicts both partial absenteeism from work and psychological strain.[11]

Cultural issues also define who the caregiver will be. Part of the stress within a client's family stems from the fact that the daughter-in-law is acting as the caregiver rather than the daughter, when the client's expectation is that this should be her daughter's role. Most older people regard their siblings as a caregiving resource, but only small percentages actually receive sibling help. Cicirelli, Coward and Dwyer[12] found that those receiving sibling help were more likely to be younger, to be divorced, widowed or never married, to have fewer living children, and to reside in small cities or rural areas. Those reporting cessation of help were more likely to be older, to have a decrease in IADL impairment, and to have changed their area of residence. The findings support the concept of a substitution hierarchy where sibling help is given when the elder has functional impairments and support from a spouse or adult children is unavailable. As almost the last resort of those needing help, siblings as caregivers were both a strong source of stress and support.[13]

How Are They Performing?   Special attention should be given to the caregiver. Caregivers have often been given, or have accepted, more responsibility than is reasonable. Spouses are often expected to care for each other despite illness or disability, twenty-four hours a day, seven days a week, without relief. The result is that the caregiver frequently becomes ill and unable to assume the burden of care, moving two people toward institutionalization that could have been prevented. When assessing the caregiver, the case manager must interpret verbal and nonverbal cues. The caregiver may deny fatigue or illness, but body language, posture, and physical signs of fatigue may be present to confirm it.

The case manager must pay attention to the type of care provided and the amount of time required for care, as well as the other responsibilities that the caregiver must handle in addition to the care provided. For example, if the required care is to assist the client with bathing, food serving, toileting, and transfer in and out of bed, the caregiver may provide about five hours of care each day. If the caregiver is frail, works outside the home, or has other responsibilities with additional family members, there is an increased chance of caregiver burnout.

The case manager should be particularly aware if the caregiver is burdened with a demented client. The client may require only supervision, but will tend to have altered sleep patterns, a loss of learned behavior, incontinence, or disorientation. This is a strain on the caregiver because the client must be watched throughout the twenty-four-hour period. Such disabilities are slow to develop, so outside supports tend to wane over time. The caregiver becomes increasingly tied down and also experiences anguish at watching a loved one deteriorate. This anguish is often accompanied by fear, anger, and/or guilt.

When planning for these clients, the case manager should include the caregiver in the planning process. All too often the client states that a neighbor or friend who has helped in the past will continue to help and the care plan is finalized without consulting the neighbor in private. Then the neighbor either refuses to participate or just never quite complies with the plan. Caregiver participation must be confirmed by the caregivers after they have had an opportunity to verbalize their feeling about what is expected of them. Many of these caregivers have difficulty telling the client that they are unable or unwilling to continue with the burden of support, but they should be encouraged to verbalize to the case manager without fear of being judged.

The case manager must be able to recognize when the client expects unrealistic support from caregivers and service providers. It is easy to inform the client who requests that homemakers provide care in twenty-four-hour shifts that such service is unavailable. However, the case manager may have a problem telling the eighty-eight-year-old, bedridden, incontinent man that his eighty-year-old wife needs help caring for him, especially if he responds that she can manage his care. Both the client and the wife need to be realistic about the burden of care.

Occupational Hazards.   There are several potential costs that the caregiver faces. The economic cost may involve not only additional expenses incurred in caring for their loved one, but also potential loss of income when a caregiver resigns or reduces hours of employment in order to increase caregiving time.

The caregiver may experience a tremendous emotional cost. The caregiver of the client with dementia may deny that there is a problem and in struggling to accept it may appear afraid both of what is happening and of what may happen in the future. Caregivers feel overwhelmed, helpless, and trapped, and express anger at the client. Caregivers who do not understand that these are common emotions feel guilty. Guilt also results from the feeling of inadequacy as a caregiver. Chronically ill clients do not get better no matter how good the care provided.

One of the most important costs may be social, in that caregivers may lose leisure time and experience less freedom to leave home alone if at all. Friendships may become strained, especially if the client exhibits memory loss. Friends who do not understand the illness tend to forget the needs of the family and deal with their feelings of discomfort by avoiding the confused client.

Assessing Social Activities

Participation in social activities should also be covered. Social does not just imply the parties or community events the client attends, it means the amount of contact one has with other humans. Visits from family, friends, religious representatives, volunteer groups, or even the lady who brings a meal at lunch all provide an opportunity for social interaction and relief from loneliness. However, the fact that social contacts take place does not mean that they are all satisfying. One cannot record the number of social contacts per week and make a judgement about isolation. The person who does not see anyone for months is isolated, but some people would find more than two or three contacts per week irritating. Others may be constantly surrounded by a crowd of uncaring and unresponsive people. Case managers will also encounter the client whose family jumps to her every wish, a situation she controls by constantly complaining that no one cares about her.

A clue to the degree of social isolation is to examine past lifestyle. A client who has chosen to live alone is very different from one whose family members have died or moved away. What the case manager considers is the client's interpretation of isolation and loneliness; if they seem content then that evaluation takes priority.

Assessing the Client's Physical Condition

The assessment normally carries information on physical health. Areas discussed may include illnesses, medications, nutrition, treatments or therapies the client is undergoing, and perhaps a risk assessment looking at behaviors such as smoking and alcohol consumption.[14] It may be difficult, particularly with a noncompliant client, for the case manager to get accurate information. Since the client's physician is usually contacted as a matter of procedure, extensive questioning in this area is not necessary. The case manager from a nonmedical background should have a basic understanding of medical terms that are common with case managed populations. Table 4.2 provides some standard definitions.

Assessing the Client's Use of Medication

Not only should the medication type, strength, and prescribed frequency be recorded but also whether the client takes it as directed. When questioning a client on this point it is important not to ask the question directly. The case manager will find it much more helpful to read the prescription label to determine the correct frequency and then ask the client how often the medication is taken. An incorrect answer will alert the case manager to a medication problem. The case manager should also determine if the client knows why they are taking a medication. If a

TABLE 4.2   **Medical Terminology Relevant to Case Management Populations**

Chronic illness:	the presence of long-term disease or symptoms, commonly a duration of 3 months or longer
Impairment:	a physiological, psychological or anatomical abnormality of bodily structure or function, includes losses or abnormalities, not just those attributable to active pathology. Severe injury can cause extensive physical and neurological damage, is extremely costly to treat in both acute and chronic phases and can have a devastating impact on an individual's social and psychological status.
Developmental disabilities:	a broad range of conditions evident at birth or in early childhood that can result in lifelong deficits in mental, psychosocial, and physical functioning
Secondary conditions:	conditions related to the main illness or impairment that further diminish the person's quality of life, threaten his or her health, or increase vulnerability to further disability
Activity limitation:	a long-term reduction in a person's capacity to perform the average kind or amount of activities appropriate to the person's age group such as going to school, going to work, and living independently
Functional limitation:	results from impairment or chronic illness and is a restriction or lack of ability to perform an action or activity in the manner or within the range considered normal
Disability:	a limitation or inability resulting from impairment or chronic illness to perform socially defined activities and roles expected of individuals in the manner considered normal

client states that he is taking a cardiac medication for nerves, it is probable that the client does not understand his physical condition or treatment.

Medication errors frequently occur when there are more than two medications taken, particularly when the client has symptoms of dementia. There may be more than one physician prescribing medication; one physician may not know what the other is prescribing.

It is also valuable to know whether the client ever gets her medications mixed up, takes someone else's medication, or has problems getting prescriptions filled. A case manager is likely to encounter people who take medications prescribed for other people; if his sister had the same symptoms, then surely her drugs will work for him also.

The case manager should investigate the reasons that a client has medications that have been prescribed but are not being taken. The reasons may be multiple and varied, such as the fear that taking medication will lead to side effects, or may be due to confusion on the client's part. The cost of medications, the time and difficulty involved in getting to a pharmacy, and/or the absence of someone to go for the client are very common reasons that the client may be noncompliant with the prescribed medical regimen.

Nonprescription medications may be as potent as a prescription medication and they may produce a wide variety of side effects. It is possible for an elderly person to abuse substances which are over-the-counter medications. An example of this is the use of laxatives by older clients, sometimes taken daily, which not only becomes a chemical dependency but leads to dehydration and malnutrition.

Finally, the total number of medications can portray an indication of the client's self-perception of their health. Heavy use of medication, particularly if prescribed by a variety of physicians, indicates a client who perceives himself as in poor health—which may not be accurate.

Assessing the Client's Diet

The client's diet is important for two reasons: dietary habits may indicate a risk to the client's health or a prescribed diet may be a crucial element in the client's medical care. One case manager visited a potential client who lived in an isolated mountain region. Because he had no transportation for grocery shopping, he had been living for months on the plants that grew wild around his home. Another client simply refused to eat anything but candy. Regardless of intent, both of these people were seriously undernourished.

The case manager should record any special diet that has been prescribed for the client, who prescribed it, and whether the client follows the diet. When a special diet is stated to be a problem by the client, it is important to find the reason that it is difficult for them. Clients may state that they cannot afford the food, that preparing the diet is a problem, or that the taste does not appeal to them. There are also clients who may decide not to follow the diet for no particular reason.

Another reason for noncompliance with a diet is the client's relationship with other people in the environment. Clients may occasionally feel that they cannot impose a special diet or special food preparation on other members of the household or the caregiver may not be willing to spend the time or money to comply.

Assessing the Client's Mobility

Mobility refers to the clients' ability to transport themselves both in and out of doors. This does not necessarily mean that one must be able to move quickly or without aid. Persons needing the assistance of a device such as a cane, walker, or wheelchair may still be totally independent and safe.

A comprehensive assessment should address the client's ability to perform their own bathing, dressing, and grooming. Joint limitations and the ability to put extremities through their normal range of motion are clearly demonstrated in the grooming process. A client's ability for self-maintenance also indicates something about self-esteem. Clients may be seen who wear excessive amounts of makeup and/or a wig in an attempt to disguise the aging process or perhaps hide the fact that they are unable to properly clean themselves.

Summarizing the Assessment

An assessment is simply a piece of paper or a computer screen with blank spaces to be filled. Its only real value is in the effect it ultimately has on improving the life of the individual. The information gathered at the assessment interview is only as good as the sources and the interviewer. Sometimes case managers feel that, since this will be their case, there is no need to write down small details or explain impressions they have recorded. However, documentation is necessary to avoid confusion among cases, if there is a shift in caseload responsibility or the case manager leaves the agency, or if there is a need to call in legal or psychological consultation.

There are a few steps the case manager can take to increase the accuracy of the assessment.

1. Following an interview, make an observation concerning the reliability of the client's responses, particularly indicating those items that seemed out-of-line.
2. Record other sources of client information, such as family members, the neighbor who came out to the car for a private conversation, the nurse who made the referral.... All of these add to the creation of a complete picture of the client's circumstances.
3. Record dementia, impaired judgment, indication of substance abuse, or any factor that might impair the judgment of the person being interviewed.
4. Record factors that might create communication limitations, such as sensory impairment, loud or distracting noises, or language differences.
5. Indicate the client's demeanor if there is an indication of a fear of answering, unexplained hostility, or a strong lack of interest.

EXERCISES

Discuss whom you would interview to assess the following cases and the topics you would cover.

1. Genevieve is an eighty-two-year-old woman who suffered a fractured hip one year ago. She is a brittle diabetic, and has gone blind in the last year from macular degeneration. She suffers from a mild heart condition, and also has compact fractures from osteoporosis. Genevieve has a daughter, Jackie, who lives with her because fifteen years ago she developed multiple sclerosis. The daughter is still able to walk but has difficulty with her vision and can no longer drive. Jackie has to do all the grocery shopping and all the care of her mother, who is also incontinent. Genevieve cannot stand the pain from her hip and keeps her daughter up all night. Genevieve also has a son who lives twenty-five miles away and suffers from diabetes. Dave expects his sister to cook an evening meal for him every night but often cancels coming over at the last minute after Jackie has already fixed dinner. The daughter has promised Genevieve that she will never go to a nursing home but is growing very tired and short tempered. The family has a limited income, and has difficulty keeping the house clean. The daughter cannot see the insulin syringes in order to fill them. Currently, a church member comes on a weekly basis and fills Genevieve's syringes. Dr. Clarke has called you as the case manager to try and help this family.

2. Tina is a twenty-one-year-old patient you have been given. She is being released from Sentara Ridge Psychiatric Hospital. She suffers from depression and anorexia. She entered the hospital weighing only eighty pounds and was placed on intravenous feedings. She currently weighs one hundred pounds, but is threatening to lose the weight again. She lives in a very unstable home environment. Her father is a traveling salesman and the mother works at a local department store in town. She has a younger sibling, who attends college. She still suffers from depression, but is not actively suicidal. She is terribly afraid of going home, and is too weak to return to work.

KEY TERMS

assessment
interview
primary caregiver

NOTES

1. Roberts-DeGennaro, M. (1987). Developing case management as a practice model. *Social Casework: Journal of Contemporary Social Work, 68,* 466–70.

2. Ramsdell, J. (1991). Geriatric assessment in the home. *Clinics in Geriatric Medicine, 7* (4), 677–693.

3. Intagliata, J., Willer, B., & Egri, G. (1988). The role of the family in delivering case management services. In M. Harris and L. Bachrach (Eds.), *Clinical case management.* San Francisco: Jossey-Bass.

4. Moxely, D. P. (1997). *Case management by design*. Chicago: Nelson-Hall.

5. Steinberg, J. A., & St. Coeur, M. (1996). *Case management practice guidelines*. St. Louis: Mosby.

6. Auslander, G., & Litwin, H. (1991). Correlates of social worker contact with clients' family networks. *Journal of Social Service Research, 14* (1/2), 147–165.

7. Pearlman, D. N., & Crown, W. H. (1992). Alternative sources of social support and their impacts on institutional risk. *The Gerontologist, 32* (4), 527–535.

8. Dwyer, J. W., & Coward, R. T. (1991). A multivariate comparison of the involvement of adult sons versus daughters in the care of impaired parents. *Journal of Gerontology: Social Sciences, 46* (5), S259–269.

9. Lee, G. R., Dwyer, J. W., & Coward, R. T. (1993). Gender differences in parent care: demographic factors and same-gender preferences. *Journal of Gerontology: Social Sciences, 48* (4), S9–16.

10. Gorey, K. M., Rice, R. W., & Brice, G. C. (1992). The prevalence of elder care responsibilities among the work force population. *Research on Aging, 14* (3), 399–418.

11. Barling, J., MacEwen, K. E., Kelloway, E. K., & Higginbottom, S. F. (1994). Predictors and outcomes of elder-care-based interrole conflict. *Psychology and Aging, 9* (3), 391–397.

12. Cicirelli, V. G., Coward, R. T., & Dwyer, J. W. (1992). Siblings as caregivers for impaired elders. *Research on Aging, 14* (3), 331–350.

13. Suitor, J. J., & Pillemer, K. (1993). Support and interpersonal stress in the social networks of married daughters caring for parents with dementia. *Journal of Gerontology: Social Sciences, 48* (1), S1–8.

14. Ramsdell, J. (1991). Geriatric assessment in the home. *Clinics in Geriatric Medicine, 7* (4), 677–693.

CHAPTER

5 The Plan of Care

Care Planning is the process of developing goals to meet the client's needs and identification of services necessary to achieve those goals. Often in the form of a contract signed by the client and case manager, the **plan of care** should state:

1. the goals agreed to by both and based on the information of the assessment,
2. time limits on the overall case as well as on the individual goals,
3. the extended actions to be taken by all parties to achieve the goals,
4. who accepts responsibility for each task, and
5. the consequences for a failure to comply.[1]

Goal Setting

Assessment information provides the basis for the formation of goals. Care planning is the link between the assessment and the delivery of services; it is the action taken to address these problems identified. For many case management systems, care planning is an exercise in resource allocation.[2] Working within restraints of funding, personnel, or time, the granting of services to one applicant means fewer or none for another applicant. Although the choice between Client A and Client B is rarely so clear cut, the knowledge that generosity in the present may lead to restrictions in the future should be a standard part of designing care plans.

The process of translation of assessment data into care plans is based on the professional judgement and practical experience of the case manager. After an inventory of needs and demands has been developed, specific goal statements are formed. These not only are required on the care plan, but they are also realistically required in order to compose the care plan. Each goal should contain an explicit criterion for success to determine the success of the plan of care.

Few areas of case management are more difficult than goal setting. The most common error is overestimating both the case manager's and the client's abilities. Goals are set that are unrealistic or vague so that no measurement can be made to determine if the client is making progress or not (see Table 5.1).

Service plans are goal directed and time limited, so they should include both long-term and short-term goals. Long-term goals state the situation's ultimately desired state. Short-term goals aim to help the client through a crisis or some other

TABLE 5.1   Writing Goals

Poorly Written Goals	Well-Written Goals
"To prevent Mary from being lonely." Everyone feels lonely at some point. This is totally idealistic.	"To provide daily contact through use of telephone reassurance program" is realistic and measurable.
"To provide personal care." Such a goal would result in a case that could never be closed because the agency could never stop providing personal care.	"To have a bath once a day" is something that can be accomplished and measured. At the point that the client or an informal resource can accomplish this task, it is no longer necessary for a formal provider to do so.

present need. Whatever the time constraints, goals establish the direction for the plan and provide structure for evaluating it.[3]

The case manager and the client may need to decide whether to focus on long-term or short-term goals. The client may be seeking immediate changes in the situation, as in crises that must be handled. Be aware that often a major part of the client's situation is that their energies are constantly being used up to respond to crises that didn't need to happen or could have been averted if more planning had been done. So clients need goals that will bring about a long-term increase in their competence or a combination of their and their helping network's competence. Only in this way will the cycle of constant response to crises be broken.

CASE EXAMPLE

Joe is a sixty-year-old gentleman who had been living with his elderly mother until her recent death. Joe was afraid the state was going to "kick him out" of his home because of the state recovery act. He has now moved closer to his sister in another part of the state.

He is currently living in an apartment complex for the elderly and disabled. Joe has high blood pressure and heart disease. He has also been diagnosed with depression and paranoid schizophrenia. Joe has a high IQ but cannot remember how to take his medications. Joe becomes anxious easily and does not have a psychiatrist near where he now resides.

On the other hand, there is a need for reinforcing successes and signs of movement that increase the clients' confidence and in turn enhance their competence and willingness to try harder. The case manager has to use thoughtful judgment in determining how much energy should be put into short-term and how much into long-term goals.

CASE EXAMPLE

David Jenkins is a thirty-six-year-old heterosexual male. At the age of sixteen he was in an auto accident that required a spleenectomy to save his life. He had fifteen units of blood at the time. This was during the time period when blood was not checked for the HIV virus. David has not been feeling well and went to his family physician. The physician, knowing David's history, decided to check him for the AIDS virus. David's test came back positive. Dr. Amos gave David the news. David is ashamed and depressed. He is suffering from a sense of helplessness. David feels emotionally abandoned. The case manager has been assigned to assist David in becoming empowered over the disease process.

Negotiating a Conflict in Goals

There will be instances when the goals of the client, the goals of the caregiver, the goals of the case manager, and even the goals of the community may not agree. Table 5.2 illustrates some of the possible issues. Each of these sources has an investment in the outcome of the change efforts. Sometimes they are in conflict with one another, or the professional providers are not in agreement with the client about which goals should take precedence, and that makes setting priorities complicated.

TABLE 5.2   **Examples of Goal Conflicts**

Client vs. Caregiver	Mrs. Ross wants to remain in the home with her daughter, who has three small children and a job outside the home. However, the daughter is insistent that Mrs. Ross be placed in a nursing home. She therefore refuses care so that she will have a stronger case for institutionalization.
Caregiver vs. Case Manager	Mr. Morton has deteriorated to the point that he requires constant skilled nursing care. The case manager has asked the family to have him placed in a nursing home for his protection. The family realizes that when he becomes institutionalized they will no longer have use of his social security income and demands that in-home care be continued.
Case Manager vs. the Community	The case manager received a referral from a city councilman who had received complaints from neighbors who think Mrs. Sloan should be removed from her home, which is filthy and overrun with dogs and their fleas. Mrs. Sloan is unable to go marketing and therefore wanders the neighborhood asking for food. The case manager judges that with the provision of homemaker services, Mrs. Sloan will be able to remain at home.

It is the belief of most case management programs that the client's goals are the most important. The client, after all, is the person the case manager is trying to serve, who often has to adapt to changes or to enact changes. Ultimately, the client is not only the one element who should be satisfied with the outcome but the one without whose cooperation the outcome cannot be controlled.

Such conflicts intensify the predicament for the case manager because in each case, a potential resource provider is resistant to the goals determined by the client or case manager. Just as a client cannot be made to accept services, so can an informal resource not be forced to provide care. After all attempts at compromise have been exhausted, the case manager must foremost consider the health and safety of the individual, even if it may not seem the most desirable solution. Table 5.3 illustrates how the previous problems were resolved.

Dealing with the Values of Goals

The stated goals of a client may seem inappropriate to the case manager. The case manager may feel that the client has expectations much higher than is reasonable; perhaps the client wants to return to a job they can no longer physically perform, resume a failed marriage, or "make everything like it used to be." Perhaps the most difficult cases are those who refuse to accept the most appropriate care.

Conversely, the case manager may believe that the client is actually capable of obtaining a higher level of success than the client believes possible; a client stating that having someone handle her business affairs would be able to do this independently if her illiteracy was addressed or another client who would like someone to read the newspaper to him each day may have improved vision

TABLE 5.3 **Examples of Conflict Resolution**

Client vs. Caregiver	Mrs. Ross and the case manager were unable to persuade the daughter to allow her to remain at home. In lieu of a nursing home, the case manager arranged for Mrs. Ross to move into an elderly apartment complex that offered an assisted living program. Mrs. Ross was able to retain most of her possessions and independence.
Caregiver vs. Case Manager	Mr. Morton's case manager determined that he was indeed at risk in the home and contacted the protective service agency so that legal steps could be taken. The court appointed a guardian who then arranged nursing home placement.
Case Manager vs. the Community	Mrs. Sloan's case manager arranged homemaker services, had the city pound collect the dog population, and had the house sprayed to kill the fleas. Two months after care had begun and the home was in acceptable condition, the case manager, with Mrs. Sloan's permission, invited the neighbors who had complained to visit. After each expressed satisfaction at the resolution of the problem, she wrote a report to the city councilman.

CASE EXAMPLE

Mrs. Johnson is a seventy-six-year-old white female, who has been admitted to a case management agency. She is suffering from terminal lung cancer and chronic obstructive pulmonary disease. She is three months post-op from a fractured hip. She lives alone in an apartment complex for the elderly and disabled. Her only relatives are distant nieces who reside out of state. An elderly friend who continues to work manages her finances.

She requires continuous oxygen, and hospice provides aides for her personal care two to three times per week. Mrs. Johnson is forgetful when it comes to her medications. She does have a Do Not Resuscitate order. At this point she is too weak to answer the door or walk to the kitchen to prepare any type of meal. The disease is progressing rapidly, and she is determined to stay in her apartment till her death.

through more aggressive medical care. For these cases, the case manager does not want to scoff at the client's expressed desires, for doing so would end any free exchange of ideas and information. However, offering alternatives which may be compromises between the lesser and the greater goals will provide intermediate steps that will either offer a success where there was little possibility of it (as in securing work in the same field but at a less physically challenging position) or offer a greater success than was anticipated (providing reading glasses as well as a reader during an adjustment period).

Goals do not come only from the client and the case manager. Different cultures judge actions in different ways. Understanding and working to coordinate these differences to protect the health and safety of the client is an important task for the case manager.

CASE EXAMPLE

Living in Virginia Beach after migrating from Vietnam two years earlier, the parents of a three-year-old boy have resisted having their son's heart valve surgically repaired. The cost of the surgery would be paid for by the sponsoring agency. The surgeon could not understand why the child's parents would not allow the surgery to take place. Mrs. Wolfe, the senior case manager, was called in to explore the reasons behind the parents' decision. Mrs. Wolfe learned that they felt the child's heart problem was the result of God punishing them for seeking a new life, and leaving many family members behind to face the new government.

Society also has expectations about desirable client outcomes. A case manager with a juvenile probation caseload must represent society's goal of remaining safe from additional crimes. If the youth achieves self-esteem, learns a trade, and bonds with his parents, which may be the case manager's goals, these are additional benefits. If the youth continues to rise in his gang, impresses his girl friend, and obtains money for a car, which may be his goals, society's goals are unmet.

CASE EXAMPLE

Ruth is a fourteen-year-old, who is four months pregnant. Ms. Barber, the school's new social worker, approached Ruth about her plans regarding the baby. Ruth tells Ms. Barber the baby is hers and no one is going to take it away from her. Ms. Barber reassures her that is not her intention, but Ruth runs away. The next day Ruth comes to her office crying and shaking. She tells Ms. Barber that she could not find any cocaine.

Case managers often must separate their own values and perceptions from the administration of care; goal setting is one instance in which this is a frequent and critical exercise. There is always the inclination to inject the case manager's personal expectations, based on personal experiences or those of other clients. Some of this tendency is due to stereotyping of people based on class, racial, or ethnic characteristics or by categorizing people by diagnosis or health status. After dealing with a difficult cancer patient, the case manager may approach the next with a sense of dread, expecting similar behavior.

Each person also brings personal values to a relationship. A case manager may believe that a certain behavior, lifestyle, or opinion is "bad"; or it may be as simple as defining "cleanliness" differently than a client. Perhaps the most difficult adjustment for new case managers to make is accepting other standards of living.

CASE EXAMPLE

Jeff came running into his supervisor's office with a look of horror on his face. As a new case manager, he had just begun his series of home visits in the rural area he had been assigned. Ms. Toothman was prepared for an account of finding a deceased client or perhaps an auto accident. Instead, Jeff gasped out the horrid conditions he had discovered in a client's home. Chickens. Three chickens. In the house. Perched on the kitchen window sill. Before Ms. Toothman could reply, Jeff was pounding on her desk that the client must be removed from the home immediately, a court order for protective custody should be obtained, and emergency nursing home placement arranged.

Jeff was much surprised when Ms. Toothman began laughing, telling him that his client had kept chickens as pets for years, that the homemaker cleaned up their droppings the best she could, and that the client had the right to set her own standard of what was sanitary as long as she was not in danger.

Working under preformed opinions to establish goals for a client creates a barrier to seeing the individual as unique and closes down creative and supportive thinking. Jeff's experience is very common among new case managers, many of whom have come from middle-class homes where the standards of living are quite different from the ones in which they are now working. Case managers have had to deal with clients who have saved every newspaper from the last decade, clients who dress formally every day, clients who never dress fully, clients who expectorate into paper cups, and those who require the homemaker to stack cans in the cupboard in alphabetical order. Some clients keep pet snakes running loose in the house, others become distraught at the slightest speck of dust. Younger clients may listen to music or watch movies that make the case manager uncomfortable. The combination of these perceptions and values makes it very easy to subtly influence a client's goals without doing it directly or even consciously. Each person may privately make a decision about the appropriateness (or weirdness) of each behavior, but the case manager should accept these as the norm for the individual and deal with them on that level—judgment free.

There are also client standards that are inappropriate to the delivery of services. Clients who refuse the services of a worker because of race, gender, appearance, or any other characteristic that, in reality, has no effect on service delivery, can be true problems. If the client is receiving case management by choice, the client may be told that unacceptable behavior will result in the termination of services. If, however, the service is mandated, the case manager or the case manager's supervisor must force compliance.

CASE EXAMPLE

Jackson was a thirty-eight-year-old man, married, with five children. Neither he nor his wife worked. Elizabeth, Jackson's wife, had a low IQ and had difficulty with parenting skills. The family received welfare and the children had an open Child Protective Service case. The previous case worker was a man, and had often gone fishing with Jackson in order to get him to cooperate. Jackson's family had been transferred to a new case worker, who was a female.

Although Jackson's wife was very receptive to the new worker, Jackson refused to cooperate because "she was a woman." According to Jackson, women didn't know anything, and he wasn't going to work with one.

Defining Goals

However, it is often necessary to assist clients in articulating what their goals are or how to implement a plan to achieve them. Simply stating that one wants to leave the nursing home is insufficient; the case manager should ask, "What would it take for you to be able to stay at home safely?," should direct the discussion to either concrete steps to be taken so that a transfer can be arranged or to a realization that sufficient resources do not exist for such a goal. There may be a thin line between assisting thinking and influencing it. No plan works perfectly, but plans that clearly spell out objectives make it easier to evaluate successes and to suggest alternatives for strategies that have not worked well.

Service Planning

There is little purpose to a lengthy assessment of client needs and resources if all care plans look alike. Case managers are expected to develop a care plan for each client, based on that client's individual needs, addressing night and day, weekend and weekday requirements. Rather than a shopping list of services, the care plan should be a coordination between the formal services and the informal support system. Effective care planning involves the careful consideration of all possible service alternatives before a decision is made regarding which is best for the client. It also allows estimates of the cost of various care plans.

The type and amount of care should relate to the goals. If the objective is to maximize self-care, the case manager will assure that as few services as possible are provided without jeopardizing the client. If the objective is to strengthen care of family, the amount of assistance should vary to fill in the gaps identified (see Table 5.4).

If the objective is to reduce the strain of an overworked family a care plan with an emphasis on respite will be appropriate. If the objective is to allow the family to adjust to a major change (such as a sudden disability) which may require a major decision (nursing home placement) the case manager should increase care temporarily to allow the family time to organize and make a carefully considered decision. The ability to provide such an array of services is contingent on the extent of community resources with which the case manager is familiar. Therefore a case manager should maintain a listing of service agencies and organizations, what services are provided by each, the eligibility requirements for those services, and the contact person in order to fulfill this responsibility.

Ballew and Mink[4] describe four methods for achieving goals. The first is to act immediately to help the client with direct service, such as teaching a new

TABLE 5.4   Levels of Service

Disability Level	Type of Services	
	Home & Community	*Institutional*
Low	home cleaning, homemaking, home-delivered meals, transportation, home health care	various forms of sheltered housing
Moderate	home help, personal care, respite care	day care, assisted living
High	home nursing, intensified services	nursing home, skilled nursing facilities, hospital long-term care

Topinkova, E. (1994). Care for elders with chronic disease and disability. *Hastings Center Report.*

mother how to bathe her infant. The second method is to link the client to resources, such as scheduling an appointment with legal services over a custody problem. Another is to use the resource to develop competence within the client to meet his own needs or the demands of society, such as arranging for tutoring for a failing student. Finally, the case manager finds resources to help the client learn how to find other resources: for example, arranging job search training and interviewing practice.

Within these progressively less-direct methods of assistance is a combination of services that the case manager can offer to the client. The case manager may find that a new client, often in a crisis situation, must be given immediate and direct care. However, it is to the client's advantage to utilize the less-direct methods as much as possible. This exercise increases independence and decision-making skills for those times when a case manager is not at hand.

Involving the Client

The case manager should trust the clients as having some sense of their needs and trust them to be able to make some wise decisions. The clients should be involved to the extent possible in decisions about the type, frequency, and duration of services, as they may be the best source of information about what they need. Such an approach places the emphasis on doing *with* not *for* the client.

The elements of confidence and trust are crucial to the planning process. Many clients, particularly those who have been "in the system" for a long period, may have great difficulty in developing either. They may have been disappointed so frequently that they expect nothing more. Actively participating in planning becomes a risk of building up expectations that will be shattered once again; therefore, they shrug at suggestions of change and may become argumentative or nonresponsive. Whether dealing with a juvenile who has been moved from one foster family to another or an elderly person who has been approved for services that never arrived, often the case manager ends up trying to repair the damage done by others.

The Resistant Client

The case manager has several choices in working with resistant clients. The case manager may take a parental role initially to get a placement or schedule services, hoping that once critical problems have been addressed a longer time can be spent trying to enlist the client in the process for further care. Or the case manager may focus on solving issues that can be addressed quickly, giving the client evidence of success and thereby changing their fatalistic attitude.

Another type of resistant client is the one who will not make personal decisions because they have no experience in doing so. They may have always had parents or spouses who handled all aspects of their lives, either through an over-paternalistic attitude or a more negative need for control. The client may have been deprived of power through racism or sexism[5] and expect others to determine their choices. Whatever the case manager suggests, they agree to. This can be just as frustrating as those clients who will agree to nothing. Sometimes such clients are seen as passive–aggressive when it is actually more a learned behavior than a clinical one. The case manager needs to start with insisting that the client make small choices ("Shall I come by in the morning or the afternoon?" "Would you rather have chicken or fish?") and slowly increase the importance of the decisions. Self-determination becomes a learned behavior.

Involvement in decisions does not mean the clients make all the choices about services. There may be cases in which the client may not feel a particular service is needed, yet it is clear that without this service the client cannot remain at home. It is not helpful to present the client with a choice if that service is a necessity. For example, assume the client is unable to cook because she forgets to turn the stove off and puts herself into a dangerous position. However, cooking is very important to her; she is proud of her cooking. If she is asked if she needs help cooking she is likely to say no. The case manager is now in a difficult position: either the client accepts assistance or she is inappropriate for the program because she is at risk in the home. Instead, the case manager should tell the client that this service will be provided and ask her to decide when she wants meals prepared and if she will help the homemaker in menu planning or in easy kitchen tasks.

Unless court mandated, clients can refuse services. A client refusing to allow a homemaker to do the cooking and refusing to accept home delivered meals requires the agency to decide whether or not to serve the client. These alternatives need to be explained to the client, in as unthreatening a manner as possible, and let the decision be the client's.

Involving the Primary Caregiver

While it is convenient and appropriate to keep the family involved in the care process, sometimes negative consequences can result. Family members may become emotionally overinvolved with the patient or physically and emotionally exhausted.[6] The case manager involves the caregiver in the care plan and gathers the caregiver's opinion on what services are needed and how frequently they are needed. The person who has been providing care may feel somewhat threatened by the presence of service providers. This is often found when providing care to a married man; inserting a woman assigned to cook and clean into the domain of the wife, even though she is now unable to perform those tasks, can cause serious problems in their marriage and with the care plan. Emphasis to the caregiver that all are working together for a common goal can be helpful in the beginning to establish this alliance. It is also important for the caregiver to understand that the services that she gives are a part of the care plan, that the arranged services are not designed to replace but to supplement her efforts.

Selecting Services

Staying with the philosophy of involving the client in the decision-making process, the selection of services should incorporate the client's input as well as that of pertinent family members. Discussing the alternative types of health, social, economic, and legal resources available within the client's geographic range and eligibility status alert the client to the universe of choice. It is, however, important that case managers express opinions on the programs they feel are most appropriate[7] and explain the reasons these suggestions are made. This would include the types, amounts, and providers that seem to fulfill the client's needs.

The case manager may be aware of providers that are located nearby or provide required transportation, those with more experience in serving similar clients, those who are more reliable or more affordable, or can adjust around frequent schedule changes. As each client has an individual set of characteristics, so too do the providers; finding the best match is a critical part of the case manager's role.

Simply assisting the client in choosing a service is not enough. Most vulnerable persons in a case management population do not have the background to understand the definition of many programs, to understand what exactly will happen, and what their responsibilities will be. Therefore, a significant part of the care planning is educating the client in what to expect.

If the client is enrolling in a program for pregnant teenagers, she may be quite apprehensive about the atmosphere and the activities. Perhaps she will be scorned for being in her condition, perhaps the other young women will know more about child care, or will be better dressed. Time spent explaining a project, or even taking the client for her first visit, will pay off in compliance and maybe even enthusiasm.

If the client is enrolling for financial aid and certain documents will be needed for proof of age, income, or citizenship, informing the client ahead of time will make the whole process go more smoothly.

The Final Product

The care plan includes all services provided, whether they are directly scheduled by the case manager, reimbursed by the case management program, nonpaid services by agencies, or informal support by family, friends, civic or church groups. The care plan should reflect *all* assistance received by the client. Often there is a time lag between plan development and the provision of services. During this period, the case manager seeks agency approval, if necessary, and arranges for services either within the agency or at another. It is also likely that there will be changes in the client's situation during this time. Living arrangements, relationships, income, and emotions are some of the factors that may change. The presenting problem may also show some alteration, or additional problems may surface. Any such changes may necessitate review and revision of the plan.

Service coordination is the process through which the case manager arranges and/or authorizes services and implements the service plan using various providers necessary to meet the client's needs. The arrangement of services is a process that should flow from the information gathered at the assessment and reflect the total picture of the client's situation. It requires more than a mechanical fulfillment of the activities set forth on the care plan. The case manager must take into account the characteristics of the client, the primary caregiver, and the community in the selection of a care provider. **Informal services** (those provided by family members, friends, or other unpaid, nonprofessional sources) must be coordinated with **formal services** (those provided by professional agencies or personnel, either for pay or as an organized volunteer effort).

Service coordination is a contract, whether written or not, between the client, the resource provider, and the case manager. A lapse in any one segment endangers a smooth delivery of care. Therefore, each party should understand its responsibility to the process. All case managers have had the experience of referring a client for a needed resource and then finding that the client failed to follow through on the referral. This can be very discouraging and there is a tendency to blame the client for being unmotivated instead of asking oneself whether or not the client was really ready for the referral. Sometimes case managers fail to get a client to agree that a problem even exists before they make a referral. The case manager thinks the problem exists, but the client may not agree, or may not think it is a very important problem.

On the other hand, it may be the case manager who fails to uphold a promise, whether deliberately or not. For example, the case manager appears at the client's home armed with forms, brochures, and smiles, and takes an application for services. To the client, this is an implied promise that, if eligible, the client will soon be receiving assistance. The case manager may only be taking the application in the event that there is a vacancy in an already full caseload. While the probability exists that the client may become active in a few months, which to the case manager may seem a short period, the client may be expecting services to start immediately, perhaps even the next day.

Even when the client is placed on active status "as soon as possible," this phrase may mean different lengths of time, depending on the situation. If the eligibility determination requires a physician's signature, add several days. If the forms are sent to a central location for financial eligibility, the case manager should add from a few days to many weeks. Then, once approved, the case manager must notify all agencies to send workers; if their caseloads are full, new aides may have to be hired, perhaps trained. If they have workers on staff, it may take a few days to arrange schedules, rearrange routes, or process internal paperwork. When the client needs a specially skilled worker, times can be stretched even more. If the client is being enrolled in a training program, it may be necessary to wait until the next session starts. Numerous clients have entered nursing homes, had acute mental episodes, been arrested, left the jurisdiction, or died waiting for services to start.

Informal Services

The process of service coordination first requires contacting the formal and informal providers to ascertain their availability. The guiding principals in the provision of services are that formal care should supplement, not replace, the informal services. It is extremely helpful that the family understand this premise from the beginning. This should not be taken to mean that anything being done by the primary caregiver cannot be provided through formal services, but, to the extent possible, the involvement of the family should be promoted to fortify the relationship of the client with the other relatives. However, the case manager should not take for granted that resources existing before other services were added will remain at the same level, or at all. For example, a client may appear to have a strong resource in a daughter who lives next door. There may even be expressions of willingness to assist with care. However, the case manager may have reservations about the reliability of such care and may choose to provide supplemental assistance beyond what might have appeared obvious.

There may already be a solid network of informal caregivers, needing the case manager simply to help coordinate their assistance. Others may have dissolved due to disagreements, stress, economic issues, or just because the needs of the client became too much for family and friends to handle. It may be necessary for the case manager to contact distant family members who are unaware of the client's condition or try to reconcile estrangements.[8]

An informal provider may have been holding on until help arrived; now that they are relieved of the feeling of obligation they will gradually or suddenly withdraw. Even if they verbally state intentions to continue care, the case manager may discover that the lessening of pressure allows their release. To lessen the incidence of misunderstanding, it is advisable to ask the provider's intentions out of the hearing of the client. This will allow a more honest answer; coercion does not lead to effective care.

Caregivers.   According to the literature that is available , over one half of adults with a surviving parent can expect to provide care to that parent at some point in the future. Parents as caregivers of their adult children is rare at any point; however, among older women with a surviving parent, parental caregiving is common.[9]

Case managers should be aware that ethnic variations exist in the role of caregivers; some cultures expect a stronger support of the frail and elderly than do others. One study examined employed caregivers by racial status. Both black and white groups had similar caregiving demands and similar levels of personal, social, work, mental, and physical strain. Their environmental support varied: black employed caregivers felt closer to their parents whereas white employed caregivers receive more assistance in the workplace. The parents of the black caregivers received more formal services, had less disposable income, and were less likely to be married.[10]

Formal Services

Arranging professional services is far more than making a referral to an agency or suggesting a list of possible services to a client. Service coordination requires the case manager to perform whatever tasks are required to make sure that the services are applied for, obtained, maintained, and adjusted when appropriate. Formal providers may also experience dilemmas that affect their ability to deliver services. Through understaffing, an agency may not be able to provide care immediately. Or a client may require an in-home worker with specialized training that the agency cannot provide. It is sometimes hard to find workers to serve clients in isolated rural areas.

In an ideal system, the case manager would be able to call a provider, schedule services, and all would proceed happily. Unfortunately, case managers quickly learn that all providers, and especially, all workers, are not created equal. Through experience the case manager will learn which homemaker provides friendly companionship but leaves a lot to be desired when cleaning. Another may leave a home spotless but prefer not to engage in conversation. Therefore, in scheduling services, the case manager may find it advisable to request a certain worker who will be appropriate to the needs of the client. Having a good working relationship with the provider agency will facilitate the ability to make such a request.

Coordination through Communication. It is important that the case manager maintains a constant relationship with providers. To effectively fulfill the responsibility the position dictates, providers must recognize the control of the case manager over the services, both in quality and quantity. The clients must realize that complaints or suggestions on the provision of care should be channeled through the case manager and formal providers need to relay difficulties with the client to the case manager. By acting as the link, the case manager can most effectively modify care or negotiate issues with access to all information. This increases the role of the case manager as a coordinator who facilitates cooperation among all parties. The development of an adversarial relationship with either the family or the provider does not profit anyone.

It is also necessary for the case manager to use the information and opinions of the providers in the maintenance of a case. Even a case manager who is in the client's home weekly will not receive the exposure to the home situation that a home care aide who bathes the client every day will have. The worker may notice signs of possible abuse, that medications have not been refilled, or detect signs of alcoholism. Therefore, it is beneficial to consult routinely with providers to receive their opinions on care.

The client will also have opinions on how well the service plan is working. In a case management system that requires weekly or monthly visits, feedback is easier to obtain. In those systems that are less intense, the case manager should be diligent in continually checking with the client to see how things are going. Simply asking if everything is ok may not achieve the level of information needed. More specific questions about what is liked or not liked about the home health aide, how well the homemaker cleaned the house, and whether the housing authority found the type of apartment wanted will bring the case manager a better understanding of the effectiveness of the care plan.

An important element to note: Some clients have been needing assistance for so long or so desperately that they hesitate to criticize the service. They would rather tolerate inadequate care or a surly worker than risk losing everything. Although the case manager should have explained at the beginning that adjustments would be made anytime the client was unhappy, reiterating this frequently will increase their confidence in being honest. At that point, it becomes very critical to correct the problem immediately so that the case manager retains credibility.

EXERCISES

Design and revise as necessary a care plan for the following client:

Sally Madison is eighty-two years old. She lives in a two-bedroom house with her son, Roger, who is fifty-six. Sally is diabetic, has very poor vision, and poor circulation. The numbness in her legs causes frequent falls, some resulting in serious bruises and scrapes. She is mentally alert.

Roger works at the meat packing plant from 6 A.M. to 3:30 P.M., but he still leaves his mother alone a lot at night. He states that with his job he cannot keep the house straight or come home to fix lunch. Mrs. Madison states that she needs Roger to help her in and out of the tub, so she has to wait until he is home in the evening to bathe.

Two months later you learn:

Roger stays out at night because he is an alcoholic and goes on drinking binges. Some nights he doesn't come home at all. The power company has sent a termination notice. Mrs. Madison says she gave the money to Roger out of her check; he must have forgotten to pay the bill.

The next month:

An in-home worker calls to tell you that Mrs. Madison's granddaughter, Sylvia, has left her husband and moved in with the household. She says she is looking for a job, but in the meantime she can help around the house. Roger is now sleeping on the couch.

Two months later:

Sylvia calls to say she has found a job from 8:30 A.M. to 5:30 P.M..

Three months later:

Sylvia has left to return to her husband. You get a call from Mrs. Madison's physician that she is not taking her medication. Roger is supposed to buy it; he is "forgetting."

The next month:

Mrs. Madison is in the hospital. She fell in the kitchen and has broken her ankle. She will be released in four days, but will be bedridden for several months.

KEY TERMS

plan of care
service coordination
informal services
formal services

NOTES

1. Roberts-DeGennaro, M. (1987). Developing case management as a practice model. *Social Casework: Journal of Contemporary Social Work, 68:* 466–70.

2. Austin, C. (1993). Case management: A systems perspective. *Families in society, 74* (8), 451–459.

3. Woodside, M., & McClam, T. (1998). *Generalist case management.* Pacific Grove: Brooks/Cole.

4. Ballew, J., & Mink, G. (1996). *Case management in social work.* Springfield, IL: Charles C. Thomas.

5. Ibid.

6. Intagliata, J., Willer, B., & Egri, G. (1988). The role of the family in delivering case management services. In M. Harris and L. Bachrach (Eds.), *Clinical case management.* San Francisco: Jossey-Bass.

7. Ballew, J., & Mink, G. (1996). *Case mangement in social work.* Springfield, IL: Charles C. Thomas.

8. Rothman, J., &, Sager, J. S. (1988). *Case management: Integrating individual and community practice.* Boston: Allyn and Bacon.

9. Himes, C. (1994). Parental caregiving by adult women. *Research on aging, 16* (2), 191–211.

10. Lechner, V. M. (1993). Racial group responses to work and parent care. *Families in Society: The Journal of Contemporary Human Services, 74* (2), 93–103.

6 Monitoring, Reassessment, and Disengagement

Monitoring

Monitoring is the process through which the case manager maintains contact on a regular basis with the client, the client's family, and the providers of service in order to ensure that the services are appropriate and meet the individual client's current needs. Goals for community-based services are articulated differently by administrators, service providers, and clients, with some potential for conflict. This raises the issue of how these goals can be harmonized and what the locus of that function should be. Even case managers may not be ideal for this purpose, because their gatekeeping responsibilities involve them in very close relationships with administrators and providers.

Judging Quality

The first, and perhaps most difficult, decision to be made is how to define quality. The initial step is to choose the goals and outcomes that are appropriate for each case and for the program as a whole. Since one of the attractions of case management is its individualized nature, it follows that the goals and outcomes for each client should be unique. It is also critical that they be modified as the case progresses and the client and environment change. Obviously, this creates a lack of standardization that may drive program administrators to distraction.

Who should develop the goals and outcomes? The previous chapter discussed the development of goals with the client and primary caregiver. However, one must also consider anyone who has an impact on the ability to reach the goals and achieve the outcomes. Therefore, if there are other persons in the home, they must be at least neutral to the changes proposed or else they will, by commission or omission, contribute to a failure. Other persons involved in the care of the client, such as physicians, service providers, and other providers not controlled by the case manager should be consulted to some degree to determine ahead of time if a problem will arise.

The types of goals will vary greatly with the client population being served. Table 6.1 illustrates some examples of goals for several typical caseloads. Many of

TABLE 6.1   Examples of Goals for Case Management Populations

Frail Elderly	Developmentally Disabled	Juvenile Corrections
Maintain functional capacity	Optimize autonomy	Prevent recidivism
Optimize independence and mobility	Improve quality of life	Increase self-esteem
Ensure safety	Reduce informal caregiver burden	Optimize educational opportunities
Prevent inappropriate institutional placement	Satisfy clients	Improve family relationships
Reduce public costs	Reduce public costs	Reduce public costs

these are not unique to the category in which they are displayed, as illustrated by the last item.

Once the goals and outcomes have been identified, a system of measurement must be developed. Several types of indicators can be used: structural, process, and outcome.[1] These **quality measures** fall across both the organization as macro indicators and the individual clients as micro indicators as illustrated in Table 6.2.

Structural measures look at the administrative system such as the number of clients in a caseload, the qualifications of the case managers and in-home workers, and the amount of client turnover. Caution should be taken to understand the normal turnover for a client population; for example, a caseload of hospice patients will experience a rapid turnover, while a caseload of developmentally disabled children will have very little.

Process indicators look at the activities performed. Oddly enough, the day-to-day activities of case managers are often the one element in care that is not documented in detail and therefore becomes difficult to describe, evaluate, and even prove.[2] One might count the number of home visits per month, the time from initial request to the formal assessment and to the initiation of services as measurable activities of the case manager and individualized processes for the clients as appropriate to their concerns—for example, if medication is being taken properly, if rehabilitative exercises are being done, or if counseling sessions are being attended.

TABLE 6.2   Types of Quality Measurements

Organizational Measures *Macro*		Client Measures *Micro*
Structural	Process	Outcomes

Outcome indicators judge the result of the care; was there a change and was it the anticipated change? These seem to fall exclusively in the client's domain. Considered by some to be the best indicator of quality is client satisfaction.

The final, and often overlooked measure of the quality of a program, is the action taken when the evaluation process has been completed. While it is necessary to identify gaps and problems, it is a useless exercise without a system for correction. If 15 percent of a juvenile correction program's enrollees run away from home, it should be the next step to determine how this number can be reduced, not simply report it and move on to the next measurement. On the individual level, if a client reports dissatisfaction with a service, how does the case manager address the issue? A successful case manager will not be able to solve all problems or achieve all desired outcomes but will take every available step to do so.

Monitoring the Client

Case managers are expected to continuously monitor the services provided to their clients. This requires ongoing contact with clients and service providers to ensure that appointments are kept and that appropriate and effective services are provided in a timely manner. The monitoring not only functions as a check on the quality of the services provided but also allows an evaluation of the client's condition to determine any changes that would require modification of the care plan, reassessment, or case discharge. This process involves several questions that the case manager should ask at each encounter:

1. Has the client's situation changed?
2. Are the referrals still appropriate?
3. Have the desired outcomes been achieved?
4. If not, is there progress toward the desired outcomes?
5. Should the care plan be revised?
6. Should the case be closed?[3]

When examining the types of populations that receive case management, it is evident that they require the service because they are unable or unwilling to manage their environment themselves. Very often this is because of the lack of structure or lack of permanence of their living situation, their economic situation, or their health. Therefore, by the very definition of a person who needs a case manager, we have identified an individual who is subject to frequent and sometimes dramatic change. It should be stressed that change may be a desired occurrence—a family is reunited, a surgery is successful, employment is secured. Again, monitoring of services helps the case manager stay abreast and be ready to intervene if necessary.

Contacts can either be by telephone or in person; face-to-face contacts provide more reliable information. Clients are more likely to be expressive in person; the case manager will know who is within hearing distance (which could very well affect the answers being given) and has the opportunity to observe both the client and the home environment.

The Difficult Cases.   When one visualizes the case management relationship, it is natural to picture the case manager as the rescuer to a difficult situation, rewarded by the gratitude and improvement of the clients. While there are many such cases, unfortunately, a discussion of case management must consider those cases in which the client provides so much interference to quality care that the time and efforts of the case manager seem futile.

CASE EXAMPLE

Harry Jessup is an eighty-year-old man who suffers from depression. The depression is something that Harry has struggled with all of his adult life. However, the depression has worsened in the last two months due to the terminal illness of his wife. Harry can no longer remember to go to the grocery store or pick up his wife's pain medicine.

Harry continually calls the home health nurses for emotional support, or to tell them his wife does not have any medication. He also tells the nurses he cannot sleep at night, and he takes Sarah's sleeping medicine to help him. He has told his case manager, Angie Baker, that Sarah was mean to him during their forty-five year marriage, and now it is his turn. He told Ms. Baker that he withholds Sarah's pain medicine to get even with her for being mean to him.

Harry calls the case manager for insignificant things, but when a real emergency arises he cannot remember to call her. Harry has now told Ms. Baker that he wishes he were dead, and he has the means to do it. He is trying to make the case manager promise that she won't tell anyone.

Monitoring the Service Providers

An agency representative must also monitor the service provider on its administrative abilities and its adherence to the contract. Requirements for certification or licensure must be verified. The complex financing structure that supports community-based services has resulted in the application of different quality assurance requirements to similar services, based on the source of their payment.

Monitoring the Case Management

Accountability.   The need for quality does not stop at the agency door; the evaluation of the case management function for one or all clients is essential to a program. Case managers must be decision makers; therefore, they must be accountable for their decisions. They need more than the technical knowledge of which form to complete, they must understand the philosophy of the process. Rather than scheduling services through a prescribed format, they often must also utilize resources creatively or even develop new ones. Above all, they must deliver case management in a responsible manner.

Accountability can be applied in the technical sense and in the ethical sense. Technically, all documentation should be completed correctly and each element should coincide with the others relating to the same function. Fiscally, accountability provides the shortest route between the source of funds and the beneficiary, with as few administrative stops as possible. The ethical considerations are in the judgements that the clients are receiving the most appropriate services for their situations. They are provided sufficient support to remain safely in the community but are not overloaded with assistance which threatens independence. The evaluation of ethical accountability is performed by comparing the program goals with the program performance.

Such assessments are routinely performed on the macro level; auditors invade the office and delve into the financial indicators to match pluses and minuses, to seek justification for expenditures and to assure that every penny can be traced. Quality control personnel will pull samples of case records to verify that the appropriate boxes have been checked, that signatures are on the correct line and that the pink, not the yellow, copy is in the record. Administrators judge the attainment of program goals by looking at numbers: "We wanted to serve 2,000 clients in this fiscal year, we did. We wanted to offer these three services, we did. We therefore have accomplished our goals."

It is essential that case managers apply these same principals on the micro level. "How accountable have I been to an individual client? Does his assessment accurately reflect his circumstances? Have I gone beyond the paperwork and really listened to his concerns? Have I used the financial resources to his best advantage? Does the documentation in his case file accurately reflect the changes in his life? And have his goals been achieved?"

Use of Resources.   The correct use of funds for a client, of course, involves the services paid for by the program, whether that service is a meal or a respite worker. An examination of the delivery of these services must include the quality of the product:

- Does it meet the requirements of the client?
- If the client requires skilled care, is the worker well intentioned but undertrained?
- Or is the program paying a higher price for a skilled worker who is not called upon to provide this higher degree of services? In either case the price paid is not appropriate for the product received.

Individualized Care.   Is the service being delivered suitable at all? There is a tendency to go into a home for an assessment, verify eligibility, and then bring out the checklist. "Today we have a special on personal care and chore services. We can give you a meal four times a week and a sitter on Saturday mornings." The client says, "Sure, I need help so badly I'll take whatever you can give me."

Case managers must realize that because a service can be provided and because a client may agree to accept it, it may not be the responsible thing to do. This occurs when the case manager begins with the services available and works backwards instead of really assessing the client's needs and then selecting resources that best address those needs. This is sometimes caused by the lack of a wide variety of choices available to the case manager. If only homemaker services are available, the case manager approaches the client from that perspective; this is contrary to the whole intent of a case management system.

Beyond the in-home services, accountability for the cost of a client should extend to the administrative function at the agency. If a case manager only gives the minimum effort, the client is not receiving the quantity and quality of case management that either the client or the funding source is paying for. If the case manager becomes overinvolved in the client's life, then the client is charged for attention that may not be warranted.

Documentation.   Like any other profession, case management is endowed with its share of paperwork. Regardless of the type of agency or the source of funds, any time decisions are made that affect the client's quality of life or even the extension of life there must be written documentation of what justified those decisions. The assessments that are performed are designed to direct the case manager into the logical areas that require investigation. Omission of sections in an assessment is a statement that the client is not worth the time and effort required to complete the analysis. Another common problem occurs after the case manager settles into a routine and begins to use general phrases to stereotype the clients. This obscures the individual strengths and needs of clients which should be reflected in the record.

When a case manager suddenly quit her job and the other workers divided her cases, they discovered only information such as "Home visit—no change." They were at a loss to understand what had happened in the cases, the clients were annoyed when asked to redescribe their situations, and the service providers had to spend time explaining the rationale for schedules. There was little accountability in this incident. Since this occurrence, the records at this particular agency have been most explicit.

Not only is detailed information necessary for the edification of other persons, it is valuable to the case manager. When reassessments are performed, it should be mandatory that all previous narratives and other recorded activities reflected in forms be examined to provide a measure of objectivity in discerning the success or failure of services to meet the clients' needs. Since case managers have frequent contacts with their clients, they may not be aware of gradual changes in behavior or physical condition unless they make long-range comparisons. To accomplish this end, a detailed and accurate set of records is required.

Community Knowledge.   The effective case manager needs managerial, negotiation, and interviewing skills and a working knowledge of community resources, medical conditions, and legal issues, in addition to a complete familiarity with the concept of case management and the target population. When a case manager walks into a home and assumes the role as the authority on all services to be received and accepts the responsibility for scheduling and monitoring these services, that case manager becomes the center of all need resolution. The client sees this person, who has come into his home on a regular basis, listened to his stories, and brought in badly needed assistance, as the source for all help. The case manager has been called the only provider in the system whose responsibility is being aware of the whole client.

Reassessment

Reassessment is the process whereby client status, function, and outcomes are reviewed according to an established time frame. Reassessment should occur at regular intervals, usually mandated by agency policy, although the length of the interval is dependent on client characteristics and needs. Although an interval of six months is considered the average for long-term care case management,[4] programs with high-risk populations may require more frequent assessment and those with relatively stable caseloads may only mandate annual reassessments with interim reviews of lesser intensity. Major events in clients' or caregivers' lives or changes in client status, such as the death of the caregiver or a major hospitalization, may also trigger the need for reevaluation.

The reassessment may involve a repeat of all activities performed at the initial assessment or a formal review of the status of the client and the services being provided. Most reassessments fulfill the dual purpose of ascertaining the continuing eligibility of the client as well as evaluating the effectiveness of the services provided.

The most suitable approach to reassessing services is to evaluate the extent to which goals have been reached. If each goal has been accomplished, then terminating services or establishing higher goals may be appropriate. If goals have not been achieved, a determination is needed as to whether the goals or services should be modified. In many cases the case manager will decide that the goals and the services are still proper and no change in the care plan will be made.

Disengagement

The closing of a case is a process of gradual or sudden withdrawal of services, as the situation indicates, on a planned basis. Although we usually speak of terminating a case, it has become popular in recent years to use the term **disengagement.** It is thought that such an expression has less finality and sounds less threatening to the clients. Whatever term is used, each case entering the case management system will at some point be closed. The actions taken before and after the decision to close has been made can make the transition either comfortable or difficult for the client, the caregivers, and the case manager.

Using Evaluation to Determine the Need for Disengagement

As we have discussed, evaluation is an ongoing process. So, too, must an evaluation be performed when determining whether services are accomplishing the stated goals or whether there is a need for disengagement. There are three levels of evaluation: effort, results, and adequacy.[5] All three have impact on the overall judgement as to the effectiveness of care.

Effort.   In order for any case to succeed, the client and the primary caregiver must provide some degree of cooperation. Sometimes an act so basic as refusing to let the home health aide into the house signals no interest in putting forth effort. Other times it is much more subtle: the client who forgets to notify the case manager about an upcoming trip out of town so that the home tutor doesn't waste a trip, or the primary caregiver who expects the worker to clean up after the whole family. At times it can be an annoyance, such as the client refusing to sign the hourly sheet of the aide without the case manager's approval every month or the caregiver neglecting to provide cleaning products; other times there can be more dangerous situations, such as the constant presence of illegal drug use by younger family members or threatening the case manager with a gun. In one case, a wheelchair bound client kept pet rattlesnakes which made it impossible to find any workers willing to go into the home.

Securing effort starts at the initial interview. A comprehensive explanation of what is required from the client and others in the home, specifying the consequences for noncooperation will negate any future claims that a misunderstanding occurred. Depending on individual agency policy and, often, the personal decision of the case manager, a number of warnings may be given before final action is taken. It may be useful to have the uncooperative parties sign an agreement, stating that if a certain negative behavior occurs again or a positive one does not, they understand the case will be closed. It is equally important that, should the undesired actions still occur, the case manager does not give them one more chance and the promised consequences are carried out.

For some clients, securing effort is all that can be expected. As previously stated, many persons receiving case management have chronic conditions which will not improve over time, regardless of services. For others, securing effort may be all that is needed. For example, a parolee who is required to attend job training and then apply for a minimum of one job per week cannot be held responsible for not obtaining work as long as the effort is being made.

Results.   For each client under a case management system, some sort of plan of care has been developed with the purpose of accomplishing goals. For a bedridden client, the goals may be the maintenance of the client's personal hygiene by providing personal care; for the young disabled client, it may be providing transportation to achieve job training. If the goals were written correctly so that they are achievable, then it is possible to evaluate the case to determine to what degree the strategies implemented reached the goals.

Using outcome to determine the fate of a case is another very important reason the client and caregivers should be included when the goals are first designed. If all the parties involved are not committed to success, if they do not agree that these goals are correct or possible, then the case manager cannot, and should not, expect a positive result.

Adequacy.   Adequacy may be the most difficult element to evaluate. The client may have expended the effort and the stated goals been achieved, but they fall short of providing the desired outcome. For example, having a homemaker clean the house may be less than adequate if the home is infested with fleas. Arranging for transportation so the elderly client can go grocery shopping is useless if there is no money for food. In many cases, the care plan will be judged inadequate when the case manager has not fully examined the client's situation or has been given inaccurate information.

Another perspective on adequacy is the possibility that solving one problem simply produced another. If a reliable caregiver determines that her assistance is no longer needed because an agency is now providing some care, her withdrawal from the situation may place the client in worse circumstances than before. Assisting a client in moving from the house in which he grew up, which is now in horrible repair, to a clean, secure apartment may bring on a loss of identity and depression.

As we look at the process of disengagement, we will take two perspectives: the administrative duties of terminating services and the personal duties of ending the case manager–client relationship.

Terminating the Case

There are several ways a case can close. Optimally, a case is closed because services are no longer appropriate. The client's situation may have improved, either physically or by the addition of outside resources. The decision to disengage is mutually agreed upon and, unless assistance is needed again in the future, the relationship is ended.

CASE EXAMPLES

Ms. Jackson was receiving care due to a broken hip. Once her hip replacement had been performed and she neared the end of her physical therapy, the physician, the client, and the case manager agreed that she could again assume her household responsibilities.

Ms. Warren had been receiving in-home services through Medicaid. Upon learning that her husband had been a veteran, the case manager referred the case to legal assistance, resulting in a VA pension for Ms. Warren. With the increased financial resources, Ms. Warren was no longer eligible for care under Medicaid.

Mr. Stewart had been receiving homemaker services to assist with cleaning and nursing visits to monitor his blood sugar. His daughter moved back into the home and, once trained, was able to perform both tasks.

It is also necessary to close a case when the client's condition or resources worsen. In such instances, the determination is made that the services that can be provided under the current program or agency are insufficient to protect the health and safety of the client or, in criminal justice cases, society.

CASE EXAMPLES

Ms. Arant was a mentally retarded young woman cared for by her elderly mother with assistance from a personal care attendant. Although Ms. Arant's condition would allow her to continue in the community with constant care, the death of her mother removed the only potential caregiver and she was institutionalized.

Mr. Cherry was an Alzheimer's victim attended by his sister. When he reached the final stages of the disease she could no longer keep him safely at home even with the large amount of supplemental care he was receiving and nursing home placement was finalized.

Following a conviction on two counts of burglary, Mr. Pearson was sentenced to five years supervised probation. As part of his probation plan, Mr. Pearson was assigned a case manager to assist him in securing job training at a technical school. Following repeated reports from the school that Mr. Pearson was not attending class and upon being notified that an arrest warrant had been issued on suspicion of grand theft, the case manager reported to the probation office that case management services were not effective in his rehabilitation and the case was terminated.

Bobby was a young adult, paralyzed in a car accident. Determined to live on his own, he had moved from his parents' house to an apartment. His mother, however, continued to worry about him and had requested personal care assistance. In the beginning Bobby agreed, but the case manager began to notice that he would not be home for pre-arranged visits and was becoming more and more unresponsive.

Finally, when it was time to perform the annual assessment, Bobby informed the case manager that he did not want assistance any longer. Although the case manager tried to persuade Bobby to continue, even try fewer of hours of care as a trial, he was adamant and the case was closed.

It is the case manager's responsibility to respond according to the situation, whether that requires a sudden withdrawal of services such as Ms. Edwards' case or the gradual withdrawal as when Mr. Stewart's daughter learned how to monitor his condition. Usually, the decision to close a case is a joint effort of the client, family, physician, and case manager. Sometimes, however, clients request termination for a variety of reasons. A number of clients are referred by others and, never having sought the service, seek to terminate it as soon as possible. They may consider it a loss of privacy or of independence; many elderly believe accepting help from a government agency is a sign of weakness or lack of character.

There is also the possibility that the client is uncomfortable, or simply dislikes the case manager. If this appears to be the reason for the requested termination, and the client is unwilling or unable to discuss the problem, the case manager can offer to arrange for another worker to take over the case. Unless there is a legal reason for case management, as in a juvenile probation or a court-mandated community commitment, the case manager cannot force the client to remain in the program. A referral to another agency should be considered, such as an adult protective service unit, or a mental health unit. The case manager should also notify other parties involved, for instance, the client's physician or caregivers, so they begin making other arrangements.

Most programs also include a cooperation requirement in order for a client to continue to receive services. When the client fails to provide accurate information or behaves disruptively, the case manager must take steps to adjust the plan of care. In some instances, it will be necessary to close the case.

CASE EXAMPLES

The case manager was always greeted at the door by Ms. Armstrong, leaning feebly on her cane and struggling with the latch. Once inside, the case manager would help Ms. Armstrong into a chair and help her with small chores, such as tying her shoes. Since Ms. Armstrong was unable to drive, the case manager had scheduled the homemaker to handle shopping and bill payment but would often run small errands for Ms. Armstrong.

While driving by the house to visit another client, the case manager observed Ms. Armstrong outside without her cane, sweeping the sidewalk without any apparent handicap. Later that month, she saw Ms. Armstrong carrying sacks from the grocery store to her car and driving away.

After discussing the case with her supervisor, the case manager made an unscheduled visit to find Ms. Armstrong answering the door without her previous frailty. The case manager told the client what she had seen and how pleased she was that Ms. Armstrong's condition had improved so much that care was no longer needed.

Mr. Hawkins was the primary caregiver for his wife. Although she was in need of assistance, he sexually harassed all workers in the home, to the point of suggesting that a female worker perform sexual acts on his wife. When confronted by the case manager, he stated that he was just reacting to his wife's inability to satisfy him and if the case manager would alleviate his need, everything would be fine. After referrals to protective services and mental health, the in-home care was terminated.

Mr. Byrd had worked his way through every personal care aide the contractor employed. He insulted them, accused them of stealing and, finally, greeted one at the door with a shotgun. The case manager, after numerous warnings to Mr. Byrd of what would happen if his behavior did not change, finally terminated the case.

Ms. Carter had been receiving in-home care for two and a half years when her physician retired and turned his practice over to Dr. Lott. Dr. Lott refused to sign any forms to allow Ms. Carter to remain in the program, stating that she was faking her illness and he, as a tax payer, would not pay for "free maid service." The case manager tried to schedule an appointment with a different physician but Ms. Carter would not agree and the case was closed.

Cases may also be terminated by someone other than the client or case manager. Although the client may wish to continue, often the lack of a feeling of empowerment will prevent them from disobeying or taking other action.

CASE EXAMPLE

Ms. Marshall was in the home of her daughter. The case manager had arranged for the client to attend a day care center and Ms. Marshall was very happy, especially after she met Mr. Martin. A romance began. The case manager was confronted by the daughter who thought it was "dirty" for the agency to encourage such behavior and withdrew her mother from the program.

The Process of Terminating a Case.   Whether the case closing is initiated by the case manager or someone else, it is important that all parties be informed that if care is again desired, the case manager will reopen the case. Many times the case manager will follow up on a case at a three-month, six-month, and one-year interval to determine if services are needed. The client (if possible) should be notified in advance of the action to be taken. Each client should be informed of the right to be readmitted to care as necessary.

There are few case management programs that are mandatory. There will be cases when the client or family member requests that services be stopped and refuses to give a reason. Once the case manager has made an effort to discover the motive, no more can be done. Persons cannot be forced to accept assistance.

A case closing may be a long process, such as the withdrawal of services one at a time until the client is off the program. This is especially necessary when the client has become too dependent on assistance and the case manager fears that sudden termination may adversely affect their condition.

The final step in closing a case is completing all documentation relating to the cause for the closure, notifying providers, and accomplishing agency paperwork to place the case in inactive status.

Terminating the Relationship

Closing a case is difficult in human services generally. The case manager has worked long and hard to build a relationship with the client and to become a significant part of the client's life. In many ways, the case manager has told the client to count on the case manager, if not for direct help, at least for support. The case manager has become an important part of the client's life. Now the case manager is breaking the implied promise of always being available.

The Client's Response.   There are several ways clients can react to this kind of anxiety. Some respond in anger and act as if they have been betrayed, while some are withdrawn and depressed. Others deal with their anxiety by rejecting the case managers and even claiming that they were never helpful anyway. Still others present case managers with a flurry of problems in order to keep them actively involved. It is necessary to balance the systems continued responsibility to these clients against the goals of their being competent to use help on their own. It must also be considered that there are other people who may need help even more.

The Case Manager's Response.   Case managers can have problems disengaging, too. Caring is an essential quality in good case managers, and ending a relationship with a client for whom one has come to care is not easy. Some clients are particularly hard to separate from; they might be characters who are unique or are especially lively or the case manager might be drawn to the client who is mildly dependent and highly appreciative. Still others see the client who is earnestly struggling but very vulnerable as one who needs their continuing protection. These are all reasonable and legitimate feelings. Professional objectivity is required so that the case managers do not visualize the clients as family and realize that the goal is to help them develop the ability to do without support.

This is especially important in a program that fosters close relationships between clients and case managers. Because the client is sweet, affectionate, and eagerly awaits the case managers visits, because the case manager is a good listener and friend, neither the case manager nor the client may wish to close a case even though an impartial evaluation may show that care is no longer needed. A routine examination of the objectives by the case manager, by a peer review, or by a supervisory review will decrease such instances.

It is important that case managers understand that there are some cases in which no change can be accomplished, or in which nothing can be done to prevent an outcome. The populations who receive case management are, by definition, at risk. No amount of homemaker services will prevent a child with AIDS from dying, no amount of personal care will keep a client requiring skilled nursing care out of a nursing home. Considering the target populations most widely served, that of the elderly and disabled, it is unlikely that a significant proportion will become young and healthy. Similarly, those who work with adult and juvenile offenders must accept that years of behavior can rarely be overcome by a few hours of case management. It is therefore necessary for the case manager to define *success* as lengthening the clients time at home and providing a comfortable environment for as long as possible.

EXERCISES

1. The sweet lady that you have always looked forward to visiting has recovered from her hip replacement and you realize that she does not meet the medical criteria anymore. When you bring up the subject of termination, she immediately begins to groan with pain. How do you handle it?

2. In addition to the normal evaluation activities of your agency, you want to know how well you are performing as a case manager and how you can improve. You decide to develop a questionnaire for your clients to complete anonymously. What items will you ask?

3. You are a case manager in a program for low-income clients. You receive a call from a coworker that she saw Mr. Ray at a local shopping center behind the wheel of a very expensive car. How do you proceed?

4. Mrs. Charles has been a client of yours for many years. She lives with her son and his wife in conditions that have always made you uncomfortable: poor sanitation, an air of unconcern, missed doctors appointments, and so on. Although you have monitored the case closely, including unannounced visits, you have never uncovered any verifiable signs of abuse or neglect. In the last month, Mrs. Charles has deteriorated rapidly and is at the point of needing fulltime skilled nursing care, which you cannot provide. However, when you have tried to discuss this with her son, he has vehemently refused to consider nursing home placement, even if you terminate the in-home care she is getting. How do you evaluate this case and how do you handle it?

KEY TERMS

monitoring
quality measures
reassessment
disengagement

NOTES

1. General Accounting Office. (1994). *Long-term care: Status of quality assurance and measurement in home and community-based services.* (Letter Report, 03/31/94, GAO/PEMD-94-19).

2. Nishimoto, R., Weil, M., & Thiel, K. S. (1991). A service tracking and referral form to monitor the receipt of services in a case management program. *Administration in Social Work, 15* (3), 33–47.

3. Woodside, M., & McClam, T. (1998). *Generalist case management.* Pacific Grove: Brooks/Cole.

4. Newcomer, R., & Arnsberger, P. (1997). Case management, client risk factors, and service use. *Health Care Financing Review, 19* (1), 105–121.

5. Ballew, J., & Mink, G. (1996). *Case management in social work.* Springfield, IL: Charles C. Thomas.

CHAPTER

7 Working with the Client

The Initial Interview

Interviewing techniques are specialized methods of communication in which the content and manner of both verbal and nonverbal messages are carefully considered. The method used by the worker to interview a prospective or active client carries significant influence on the accuracy of the information received and the depth of the relationship between the worker and client.

Unlike a casual conversation, an interview is conducted in order to elicit predetermined information. For the purpose of a case management system, the information is needed to determine the appropriateness of the referral to the program, the client's needs, and what resources already exist so that a plan can be developed. It is therefore a goal directed activity.

Beginning an Interview

The first impression the client forms regarding the credibility of the case manager and the program will influence all subsequent communications. It is therefore very important that the initial contact be conducted in a manner that will facilitate a positive reaction. The client must first understand the purpose of the interview. This requires a clear understanding of who the case manager is, what agency is represented, what services are offered, who made the referral, and why.

The client will have come to the attention of the case manager in one of three ways: the client may have requested case management services, someone else may have referred the client to the agency, or the service may have been offered as part of an outreach program. In some instances, the client will be ordered to accept case management as part of a treatment or rehabilitation effort. No matter how the two parties got together, the case manager will have to do two things in the first interview: introductions must be made and the nature of the problems to be worked on must be determined. The case manager should take the initiative in the introductions and as part of the introduction provide a brief description of the case manager job.

An introduction should explain several items:

1. The case manager's name and agency
2. A brief idea of what the case manager and the agency do
3. Who sent the case manager and why
4. The financial implications of the program
5. A simple description of the procedure

CASE EXAMPLE

"Mrs. Johnson, my name is Beth Elliott. I work for the Bay County Area Agency on Aging. My job is to meet people who are having trouble managing alone and see if we can give them some help. Mrs. Roberts, your niece, called and said that you have difficulty in getting your housework done since your stroke. I thought we might talk about what kind of help you want and come up with some ideas on getting someone to come in and give you a hand."

Mrs. Johnson agrees that she needs assistance.

"Our program can provide several different types of help. This program is paid for by Medicaid, so it won't cost you anything and it won't affect the amount of your check or your food stamps. What I need to do now is to ask you some questions about yourself. Then we will decide exactly what type of help you need. I will come by each month to visit and make sure everything is going well. You can also call me any time you have a question or a problem."

The case manager also builds the basis for a relationship by:

1. Establishing that she is a professional.
2. Stating that she is there in a supportive capacity.
3. Expressing (several times) that she and the client will work together to solve the problem.
4. Assuring the client that she will continue to monitor the case and be available for assistance.

If the referral came from a third party, the client needs to know who has requested services and the reason. Above all, it is necessary that clients grasp the purpose of the visit and have a basic comprehension of what a case manager can and cannot do for them. These same principles apply to interviews the case manager may have with family or professionals involved in the case. These explanations do not need to be lengthy or complicated, nor does the case manager need to apologize for being there. Language should be simple and avoid the use of jargon such as acronyms for agency names. It is not necessary to go into detail on the various duties that a case manager performs.

If the client sought out case management, then the case manager needs to be sure that he has a good understanding of the type of service provided; the client may not completely understand what exactly he has requested. If he has been referred by someone else, the case manager may have to correct misunderstandings or fill in vague understandings about the case manager's job. If the case manager has sought the client out, it is important to explain why.

Building a Relationship

Putting the interviewee at ease will make the whole process more pleasant and significantly improve the validity of the responses. The client is likely to be fearful, even when prepared by family. They are often afraid they will say something wrong and will be denied help, the caregiver will get revenge, or they will be put out on the street.

An interviewing technique illustrated in the previous example is the manner in which the case manager begins by talking about herself rather than questioning the client immediately. This allows the client some time to assess the case manager before she begins to discuss herself. The case manager is also saying that she is willing to give of herself before she expects anything of the client. This can be a very reassuring message to a person who is unsure of herself or very reluctant to ask for help.

Many of the elderly and disabled targeted by case management systems have already been through the bureaucratic mazes of various programs; many times assistance was promised and never delivered or delivered poorly. It is understandable that these persons will be suspicious of another social worker with another list of questions for another program. Therefore, it is wise to allow some time for the client to measure the credibility and sincerity of the case manager. This description should not be elaborate; the case manager should be able to provide it in a minute or two. Something simple and general will do, like "I work with people in nursing homes who are experiencing problems. My job is to help sort out what the difficulty is and to help you and the home find a solution. Later, I can help make sure that things continue to go smoothly." A case manager's job is much more complex than this but one doesn't need to give all the details in the first two minutes.

One technique is for the case manager to tell stories about other clients. Providing that confidentiality is respected, this is a great way for new clients to understand the role. It not only gives them an idea about the nature of the job, but also gives a sense of optimism by allowing them to identify with a past client whom the case manager was successful in helping.

Another aspect of the case manager's introduction involves looking for common ground. As two strangers get to know each other, they look for similarities —people they know, places they've been, things they've done. The client may be hesitant about asking the case manager about himself, so an open attitude provides this opportunity. The case manager shouldn't feel that he has to expose his private life but should look for things that he might have in common with his client and mention them briefly.

There may also be difficulty in beginning with a client who feels embarrassment because of their dependency. The case manager spends her working hours with persons at similar levels of disabilities and accepts them automatically. But to the client who must admit to others (and to himself) that he is no longer capable of performing simple personal tasks, it can be very uncomfortable to relate the problems to a stranger with a briefcase. In these cases, it may take a longer time to relay the accepting attitude that a case manager should exhibit.

The case manager will also be dealing with persons who have had little experience with government agencies. They can be suspicious, condescending, hostile, or defensive that, after all these years of managing in the middle class, they are now at the mercy of a deteriorating physical condition they can't handle, and now the government has gotten involved. Portraying an air of concerned professionalism can defuse some of these attitudes.

On the other extreme, the client may be well experienced in dealing with government agencies or the legal system. This population has a solid mistrust of anyone representing authority; responses may vary from unresponsiveness to open hostility to complete lies.

Creating a Trusting Relationship

Accepting the client and the problem involves making a client feel safe with the case manager. Clients need to feel comfortable in the relationship, to know that the case manager doesn't think them bizarre, wicked, or disgusting. Therefore, responses to clients' statements of problems or need must be nonjudgmental.

The tone of the interview may be more influential than the words used. In order to appear helpful rather than controlling, many workers use verbal communication devoid of any emotion. This robot response can lead to a sterile atmosphere which makes the client–case manager relationship too formal. At the other extreme, injecting too much emotion leads to distrust and often comes across as being accusatory, patronizing, or just fake.

The case manager should never try to negatively manipulate the parties. Trying to trick them with abrupt, rapid, or accusing questions will put them on the defensive and negate any positive relationship. Using questions to help the client express feelings and understand the situation and allowing enough time for them to form their responses will produce better results.

Clients can appear to become defensive, with statements such as "It's none of your business," "I know but I won't tell you," or "Read all those papers—they'll answer your questions." However, remember that sometimes these are techniques of persons with senility that are used to cover up the fact that they can't remember, or it may indicate that the client is under the influence of alcohol or a drug.

Creating a Professional Image

It is important to remember that people who experience multiple problems in their lives tend to think of life as somewhat chaotic and disorganized. For this reason, they need to believe that the case manager is organized. They cannot rely on someone who is as bad off as they are. Forgetting to return calls, forgetting their name, coming back to get information neglected during the first interview, or not having the correct paperwork or a pen do not give a comforting impression. If the case manager is caring enough, many people will forgive some disorganization but a lack of confidence will hurt the relationship, no matter how nice a person the case manager is.

A case manager should never call a client by his or her first name unless asked to do so; rather than making the case manager seem friendly, it makes the client feel inferior and causes resentment. Too many times the elderly, the disabled, the poor, and other vulnerable populations are treated as if they were children. As a professional, the case manager should assure that they are treated as competent adults, whether or not they are.

Physical contact such as a handshake or placing a hand on an arm is fine, often it can be used to bring a wandering conversation back to the appropriate topic. Many elderly clients want to hug when the case manager visits. But contact of this level should always be initiated by the client.

Body language of the case manager is important. A comfortable relationship cannot be built with a case manager who looks uncomfortable. Rigid sitting positions, hiding behind a clipboard, rarely looking up, and doodling while a client is talking do not give the impression that the client is seen as an individual and that the case manager is genuinely concerned with his or her situation. To avoid interference from invalid communications, the case manager should speak loudly and clearly, avoid jargon, maintain eye contact, and know when to be quiet (see Table 7.1).

TABLE 7.1 Nonverbal Communication

Positive Nonverbal Communication	Negative Nonverbal Communication
A relaxed expression	Tensing and wrinkling forehead
A relaxed smile	Pursed, tight-lipped mouth
Breathing deeply	Swallowing repeatedly
Looking interested and accepting	Clearing your throat repeatedly
Eye contact	Insincere or inappropriate smile
Reflecting your true feelings	Wetting your lips
An air of self-confidence	Staring fixedly
	Blinking rapidly
	Avoiding eye contact
	Shifting head and eyes constantly
	Squinting

Handling Personal Emotions

Mention should be made of the effect the client–case manager relationship can have on the case manager. Case managers who rotate through a caseload, listening daily to accounts of pain, disability, disease, and hopelessness run a risk of absorbing some of this suffering as part of their own bodies. There is also the constant presence of death, particularly with a caseload of elderly. Illness and nearing death force one to think and exist in the moment rather than the future; case managers who adopt the characteristics of their caseload can focus on present-centered issues, with emphasis on the tenuousness of life.[1]

Problems can also arise when the case manager has negative feelings about the client. Regardless of how humanistic one is, there are still some individuals who evoke fear, anger, or dislike. Sometimes this reaction is the result of having had a number of similar clients in the past and associating those problems with this client. Others may be entirely original and their personal, moral, or behavioral habits are either offensive or bizarre to the point that the case manager is repelled. Sometimes, once the initial shock is over the relationship can develop; sometimes there is no hope of a helping relationship and the case manager should ask to have the client transferred to another caseload.

Defining Needs

Once the client comprehends what the case manager will contribute to the relationship, it is appropriate to begin to investigate what the client needs from it. The first step in **defining needs** is to ask the client what those needs are. "What are the main reasons you made this appointment?" "Is there anything else you'd like to discuss?" Some persons are able to relate clear, realistic needs but others may be very handicapped in their ability to talk about their need for help. Others may have a general idea of their problem and only require clarification. The rest may deny any problem, either from pride or refusal to accept their dependent status.

Because most clients are not sociologists or practicing physicians, they will undoubtedly state their needs in a manner less professional than would be found in textbooks. They may also have difficulty in seeing the relationship between events. For example, a client may state the need to have someone clean the house, which has a foul odor. But the odor may be caused by the client's inability to bathe or by incontinence. It is not appropriate to be confrontational during the first interview or perhaps even the first several; the case manager should accept what the client reports and begin making his or her own evaluations.

Those with backgrounds in counseling are aware that there is a *presenting problem* and there is the real problem. Most elderly and disabled persons experience multiple problems, only a few of which the case manager may be able to affect. It is much more common for the client to acknowledge some obvious or superficial problem as a way of testing the case manager's reaction. If the reaction is favorable, then a discussion of more serious problems may follow. Other clients may try to act as if they have no problem at all. When the topics deal with subjects that most people, particularly the elderly, find embarrassing to discuss, such as unattended incontinence, it will take a deeper relationship before the client is sufficiently trusting to discuss issues that are considered too personal.

What problems the client chooses to share with the case manager at the beginning of the relationship may not be nearly so important as the case manager's reaction. In response to the client's statement of need, no matter how superficial, the case manager must do two things: acknowledge that the need is real and legitimate, and convey an acceptance of the client as well as the problem. The case manager may not agree with the client's way of stating the need but should keep in mind that the client is sharing a perception of his or her life. At this point, the case manager will know nothing about that life and is not in a position to correct or criticize that perception. The case manager can expand on and enrich the problem definition later if necessary. Even those clients who can list their difficulties are likely to report only those problems that are obvious.

Nevertheless, the interview has to start someplace. One good place to start is with the referral for service. The fact that the case manager is talking to the client means that someone thinks the client needs help. If the case manager initiated the contact, there must have been some reason for doing so and now is the time to explain it. The referral source should have provided some idea of the problems the client is experiencing. Cognizant of the fact that the source may not accurately perceive the situation, it is still a base from which to begin.

Getting Responses to the Questions
You Thought You Asked

Persons involved in a communication should understand one another. The burden of assuring this understanding rests with the professional. Planning can avoid wasting time, misunderstanding, and barriers to future communication. Before interviewing a client or a caregiver, the case manager should predetermine the points to cover. It helps to anticipate the possible responses and where the conversation should go from each one. As one gains more experience, this mental activity becomes routine but all case managers should be aware that unique situations have a way of popping up when they are least expected.

Skill in interviewing should never include negative manipulation of the other person; rather, the case manager can use questions that help the client to express feelings or understand the situation. Questions that aim to trick the interviewee or are abrupt or accusing are unproductive. Fast-paced interrogation type questioning is apt to place the person on the defensive and do nothing to establish an ongoing relationship of trust. Open-ended questions are more successful in soliciting useable responses—not much information is shared with a yes or no. "You keep scratching your legs. What's wrong?" "What do you want me to do for you?"

The content of the interview itself can lead to disclosures by an observant interviewer. When asked his age, a client might respond, "Guess," or "Older than you," or "Over twenty-one." This might indicate memory loss or lack of education.

The case manager might ask for the date of birth since this information is not as affected by senility. In some cases, the client honestly may not know his or her age because of lost records or a changed age in order to begin work before they were legally qualified.

Difficult Interviews

In those instances when the client is physically unable to be interviewed or is unreliable because of mental impairment, caution should be exercised in the use of other sources. Bias or prejudice, faulty recall, and knowing misrepresentations may distort the accuracy of information from others as well as clients.

At times the case manager may only get a long period of silence. This may be due to several causes. The questions may not have been heard. The client may not want to hear. They may not be interested in the topic. They may be thinking or remembering or deciding on the next thing to say. Or they may be tired and have no energy left for conversation. So the case manager gets uncomfortable and tries to fill the silence with chatter. Instead, the case manager should address the problem and ask: "You seem so quiet today. How are things going?" or "You didn't answer me. Are you able to hear me?" Also, remember that some silences are good. Accept tears and sadness without speaking. The touch of a hand may be the best response.

Sometimes, no matter how hard one tries to be caring and facilitative, all one gets is one word responses with no interest. Case managers should recognize that it might not be a good time for a visit and set another time. (Hint: Ask if they are missing their favorite soap opera or baseball game.) Or the client may be depressed, suspicious, or unable to follow the conversation. There are some people from whom an interviewer will never be able to get valid information; only collateral contacts can be used.

Discussing Health and Physical Complaints

Questions about physical health may occupy a segment of the discussion. When a client says "I hate to complain, but…," the case manager should be prepared for a long list. Rarely will the client offer a medical history in chronological order, providing accurate details of each incident.[2] The attitude expressed about their physical condition can also give clues. Statements like "This is what happens when you get old," or "At my age, there's no hope" can indicate depression.

A client may exaggerate his or her inability to perform because he or she wants more attention. A lady who can whiz around on her walker but says she must have someone come in to fix breakfast may just be lonely. Or the man who limps horribly when he knows he's being observed may just enjoy not cleaning house.

Sometimes, when asked for a medical diagnosis, the client will respond, "My doctor won't tell me." It is possible that the doctor did and the client will not accept what was said. Or they may deny problems because they are uncomfortable with being dependent or cannot accept their physical limitations.

Discussing Family Information

Questions about family can reveal a lot. A client into manipulation or guilt may reply: "They want to put me away so they can forget about me," "I'm a burden," "They don't have time for me," "I've lived my life, it's their turn." If family members are within earshot, chances are the client is playing a manipulation game. These can also be signs of depression.

If a client says, "they never call," when in fact the family stays in constant contact, then perhaps the client is trying to become even more dependent on them. Or they may honestly not remember recent contacts due to memory loss.

The accuracy of communication within a family can vary from joint decision making—"We discussed this and decided"—to different reports of the same occurrence. Interestingly enough, grandparents and grandchildren give closer accounts than do the adult children.

Judging Other Relationships

Having friends has a whole different meaning to the elderly. Most of their old friends have died and they become afraid to make new ones that they will also lose. Many times they will spend time with others without an emotional investment to avoid this grief. Some elderly refuse to associate with peers as a means of denying their own age—"They're all too old."

The relationships with caretakers, both informal such as family or professional personnel, can be tricky. If the homemaker is doing something wrong, the client doesn't complain. They want to be cordial, they are afraid that services will stop, they are afraid the homemaker will get revenge, but underneath there is an anger at being dependent on anyone, and especially on someone who is not living up to their expectations.

Many times the client will lash out, either loudly or subtly, at the homemaker, complaining about them personally or their work. This may be anger at the situation, not the homemaker personally. When a client goes through a whole staff of homemakers without accepting any, this may be the reason. They also may fear that their privacy is being violated. They hide things from the homemaker or may get paranoid at conversations between the homemaker and the case manager. A key to watch for is when the client quizzes the homemaker about other clients; the client may be testing to see how discreet the homemaker is.

In a household with a married couple, the wife can become suspicious of the relationship between a female homemaker and the husband. Either she is flirting with him or he is flirting with her. Unfortunately, there have been cases where this was occurring, so the accusation should not be rejected out of hand. A change in the homemaker is about the only way this can be handled. If it keeps happening, the husband is obviously initiating the advances or the wife is dreaming them up. In either case, a frank explanation to them both that services will be pulled if this behavior continues, will resolve the situation one way or another.

The final blow against the homemaker is an accusation of stealing. This may be a coverup for the tendency of the clients to lose things, or a family member who steals. Or it may be a very quick way of getting a new homemaker. A client may accuse the staff of physical abuse and have the bruises to substantiate their claim. But they may actually not want anyone to know that they tried to get up alone and fell.

Assessing the Responses

Judgment must be made as to the reliability of answers, not only from the client but also from other sources as well. Bias, prejudice, mental impairment, or even intentional deceit will negate any chance for a valid assessment of the situation. Therefore, statements should be evaluated for the possibility of a motive to be less than truthful.

A critical point when dealing with clients exhibiting chronic conditions is that what may appear obvious may not be true at all. The following two case examples illustrate this point.

In the first instance, what was assumed to be strictly a physical condition was actually precipitated by a mental condition. The second example shows how this can work in an opposite direction.

CASE EXAMPLES

Sandy had been Mr. Barbieri's case manager for years. He lived in a senior apartment complex and her visits with him usually took place in his living room. She was becoming concerned because he did not seem to be recovering from a blood infection; he was losing weight, seemed confused and listless. Her contact with the physician confirmed her fears; she was told that the medication had been changed and strengthened several times with no improvement. The doctor was at a loss to explain why no improvement had taken place.

On one visit, Mr. Barbieri was sitting in the lobby of the apartment complex. Since he seemed tired, she suggested they talk there rather than asking him to return to his unit. Sandy was amazed when Mr. Barbieri began telling her of the men who lived in his ceiling and poisoned his medication when they thought he wasn't looking. He chuckled as he told her that he had outsmarted them by pouring it down the sink when they weren't looking.

Sandy asked why Mr. Barbieri hadn't told her about the men before; he patiently explained that they overheard all conversations in his apartment and, of course, he didn't want them to know that he knew they were there.

After a quick call to the physician to explain what she had discovered, Sandy arranged to have Mr. Barbieri's medications kept at the complex office where the ceiling men could not tamper with them. He readily adhered to his medication schedule and began to physically improve.

John was a mental health case manager who had been assigned the case of Mrs. O'Brien. A woman in her sixties, she had been referred to the center by her daughter. The case notes John read described paranoid behavior—any conversations that did not include her, she interpreted as plotting against her. She had become hostile to her family and friends, accusing them of planning to "send her away." Treatment thus far had included a battery of psychological tests, counseling, and some mild anti-anxiety medications but nothing seemed to help.

Arriving for his second home visit, he interrupted Mrs. O'Brien watching television. He tried to converse with her but realized the volume was too high for comfort. This triggered an idea and he asked her about any hearing difficulties she was having. Although she denied any impairment, John found that if he lowered his voice she had problems understanding.

An evaluation by an audiologist confirmed a severe loss of hearing in one ear and moderate loss in the other. The disability would have limited her ability to hear normal volume conversations and interpret them as whispering. When it appeared that everyone around her was obviously concealing their words, her paranoid feelings were understandable. A hearing aid not only corrected her physical limitation, it improved her emotional state.

Understanding of the content of the interview is necessary on both sides. By observing the client and the environment, the case manager can make basic judgments on how well communication is occurring. Are the answers of the client being affected by the presence of a relative or in-home staff in the room? Does the client have a hearing impairment that distorts his understanding of what is being asked and therefore responds with invalid answers?

Establishing Credibility

Sometimes the client will give the case manager real answers and they are ignored. From a feeling of powerlessness to correct a problem, the case manager may try to placate the client's concerns. However, simply telling a client that things will be better tomorrow doesn't solve today's problem. As human service professionals, case managers are of a sympathetic nature; if someone is distressed, there is an urge to make them feel better. But such a response can lead the client to believe that the case manager is negating the importance of their problem. Conversations are ended with comments such as, "Oh, you'll get over it," "You'll just have to make the most of it," "You'll be better tomorrow," "Look at the bright side," "Enjoy it while it lasts," or, "Is that all?"

Positive responses can lead to greater disclosure and better **client–case manager relationships.** When someone cares, isolation is decreased. The case manager has satisfied the client's self-esteem by focusing on the client rather than on outside events. There is nothing more soothing than to know someone is really listening to you.

A case manager should never lie to a client or anyone else as a case manager. Rather than pretending to know information, it is much preferable to say, "I don't know." If the case manager makes promises of services, referrals, information, or a phone call, they should follow through. The client must trust the case manager; credibility is essential to that end.

Understanding the Client Population

These difficulties of giving and getting help are common to many situations. They are particularly acute, however, among persons who need case management services. This is true for two reasons. First, people who need case management services frequently have multiple problems that they have experienced over a long period of time. Their need for help is greater and so their vulnerability is greater, making them more sensitive. Second, they may have had some life experiences that have soured them on ever getting and using help effectively.

CASE EXAMPLE

Sally is a forty-six-year-old female who suffers from Marfan's Syndrome. She is chronically depressed, in chronic pain, and is socially isolated. She lacks family support. Sally has two daughters, one is married and the other attends college and works fulltime. Her illness is terminal. She was being seen in a pain clinic but was discharged for misuse of her medications. She is now drug dependent. She found another physician to treat her after the pain clinic discharged her for misuse of her meds. Sally is a heavy smoker, and during the misuse of her medications, dropped a cigarette in her lap and suffered second degree burns. She is paralyzed from the waist down due to a surgical procedure to repair an abdominal aortic aneurysm. Sally has completed a detoxification program, but remains depressed.

As a result of these past experiences, clients may: acknowledge problems readily and only indirectly express their negative feelings about getting help; acknowledge a need for help, but only for superficial problems; acknowledge serious problems but feel that they should be able to handle them alone; or passively cooperate in the process of getting help, and fail to follow through on suggestions, advice, and referrals.

Clarifying Expectations and Unrealistic Expectations

In addition to the negative feelings associated with helping relationships, there is another major source for confusion and conflict. There may be a misunderstanding about what is expected of the client, informal caregivers, and the case manager. Without clear role definition, the client or caregivers may be perceived as being uncooperative.

CASE EXAMPLE

Diane Watson, case manager, had completed a detailed assessment on Mr. Slavin. Because his mobility was severely limited by arthritis, he had moved into the home of his daughter, Katherine. Since Katherine worked during the day, they were seeking assistance with his personal care and to fix him a light lunch.

Diane scheduled an hour of personal care each weekday morning and two hours of homemaker at noon. She explained to Mr. Slavin and his daughter that the homemaker would prepare a lunch, clean up the kitchen and bathroom and his areas of the house. The client and caregiver were very grateful for the assistance and services started.

Several months later, Diane made a home visit while the homemaker was there. At first the homemaker told her everything was fine, but later mentioned that it took more than two hours to clean. Upon investigation, Diane learned that Katherine was leaving the dishes from the night before in the sink for the homemaker, had told the homemaker to vacuum the whole house, and to do all the laundry "since she was running a load anyway."

Diane's first reaction was anger. How dare the Slavins take advantage of this service! Her first instinct was to write them a terse warning letter but her supervisor suggested she just talk to them first in case there had been a misunderstanding.

During her conversation with Katherine, Diane realized that she had told them the homemaker would clean the kitchen. She meant that only the lunch dishes would be washed, but she hadn't stated it clearly. There was also confusion over what areas of the house were included. Diane had meant Mr. Slavin's bedroom and perhaps around the lounge chair where he spent most of his time in the living room. Again, these restrictions had never been outlined.

There may also be a miscommunication about the case manager's role. If the client has received some sort of assistance before, it is likely he will assume the new case manager will perform tasks to the same degree, if not the same end. Perhaps one of the most common misperceptions of the case manager's role is that of guardian angel. The case manager has magically appeared at the door (they are not sure who sent them) and said they would solve all of the client's problems. Now the client does not have to worry about nursing home placement, does not have to worry about paying the electric bill, does not have to worry about reapplying for food stamps. The angel is here to handle everything. Obviously, celestial credentials are not required for employment as a case manager and all will fall short of these expectations.

CASE EXAMPLE

Angela Dunson is a sixty-year-old female who had been institutionalized since she was sixteen. She had been placed in the state mental institution by her mother because she had become pregnant. Following deinstitutionalization she moved in with her brother, but he has recently died.

Angela's daughter lives close, and checks on her frequently, but she remains very lonely and unsure of herself. Angela has become very dependent on her caseworker, Ms. Shuttlesworth. She has required assistance from the case manager in pumping out the septic tank, getting groceries, and her latest request is to buy shoe strings.

Ms. Shuttlesworth has spoken to the daughter about spending more time with her mother. However, the mother–daughter relationship is strained, and the daughter finds spending time with her mother difficult. The case manager finds it difficult to limit the relationship with Angela.

Some clients will not easily relent. They will call, sometimes daily, to give the case manager a list of things to accomplish. Some of the more enterprising hunt down the case manager's home phone number so they don't have to be out of touch for sixteen hours. Sooner or later, the client will realize that the case manager has "failed" them. At this point he or she may simply terminate services early because of dissatisfaction with the service. If the assistance is too critical to lose, he or she may request another case manager, or become withdrawn or hostile.

To the case manager, this case has been a nightmare. What seemed to be a simple case has become like harassment. First, the client calls day and night with unreasonable demands, then becomes hostile, wants the case manager replaced, and is threatening to close the case. Rather than encouraging the client to do so, the case manager should examine how such unrealistic expectations developed and try to renegotiate their relationship. One method for clarifying expectations is the use of a service agreement. The service agreement is the formal expression of the understanding the case manager and the client have about the nature of their work together.

Interviewing the Elderly

There is a tendency for the young and healthy to perceive the old and frail as a different species. Their appearance and behavior is so different that there is an awkwardness in dealing with them. We begin our happy little chat, trying to keep them happy and no important information is gathered. We've been trained to only ask polite questions, especially of our elders. Those who start work in a food stamp office can be uncomfortable when they have to ask people how much money they make. Child support workers find themselves asking a woman how many men she has had sex with. Dealing with the elderly runs us into those same walls. However, if both the case manager and the client understand why this information is necessary, it can be easier to get through.

Making Contact

The case manager needs to determine that the client's physical and emotional states do not interfere with communication. The client should be asked if he or she can hear you clearly; does he or she need a hearing aid adjusted? Ask if you can be seen easily where you are. Turn off the TV, keep your hands away from your face, and make sure light doesn't shine in the eyes of the client who is hard of hearing, who might need to see your expressions and perhaps read your lips.

Look at the client. Is he slumped in his chair? Does his face register good humor or pain? Is he very rigid or relaxed? Does he keep looking away from you? There is no rule that says the elderly have to answer anybody's questions, especially when they think someone is wasting their time or invading their privacy. Ask if he'd rather go into another room for a visit; he may feel more secure to talk freely in different surroundings.

Avoid information overload. Speak slowly, using short sentences, one thought at a time, and ask for feedback to be sure the client has understood. An older person may need more time to respond than a younger adult so give them the time necessary to form an answer. If the client appears to not understand, try rephrasing the statement. Avoid arguments—even if you win, you lose. Do not be condescending. If you don't understand, ask for an explanation.

If a client is abusive or combative, check if there's a reason. Is she hungry? Did she sleep? Has her medication run out? Listen respectfully, try to clarify the complaint, and respond without being defensive. Try to remember that rarely is the anger directed at you, you are just the most convenient and perhaps the less threatening target.

Terminating the Interview

How much information is enough? Sometimes a case manager is insecure and goes into lengthy information hunting to get support. This is usually cleared up with the confidence that experience creates. One learns the major points to always cover and those that pertain to certain types of situations. As long as the door is left open for the client to bring in unexpected information, there is a good probability that enough material has been collected. The other extreme is when the case manager is busy and makes quick judgments based on early impressions and stereotypes or categorizes a case. Each client is different, each nursing home is different, each staff member is different. The case manager should be confident that enough information has been collected to know what these differences are.

One of the most thoughtful things a case manager can do when coming to the end of the time with a client is to prepare them for closure. When the conversation is winding down, the case manager says that a few more minutes remain and asks if there is anything else to discuss. When it comes time to leave, she leaves. This communicates that she is dependable. The case manager may take advantage of the opportunity to touch the client, either through a polite handshake (being careful with arthritic hands), an arm around the shoulder, or holding his hand as she says goodbye. If she will be returning, she will let him know when and why.

Working with the Caregivers

Families have always cared for their loved ones at home. What has changed in recent years is the demand for this type of care and the strains on the **caregiver.** With the emergence of managed care in both public and private insurance programs, shorter hospital stays have resulted in more clients being sent home while still needing medical care. In most cases, this must be provided by a family member. Women, who traditionally have been the primary caregivers, are now in the workforce as often as men.

Some caregivers provide service twenty-four hours a day in their homes; others provide care after work and on the weekends. One fifth of those receiving care live in the same household as their caregiver.[3] Having additional family members in the home may lend caregiving help but may also increase the daily burden.

It is estimated that one in four American households contains someone caring for an elderly relative.[4] Of the 2.4 million severely impaired persons who reside in the community, 80 to 90 percent are cared for by family members.[5] As the over-sixty-five population continues to rise, so will the need for caregiving.

It is important to remember that not all care recipients are elderly; more than one third of caregivers are providing care for individuals who are not elderly.[6] Caregiving for a child may become a lifetime commitment.

The length of time caregivers perform their role is very interesting. One study found that 36.0 percent of the caregivers surveyed had provided care for over ten years. In contrast only 5.6 percent had been caregivers for less than one year. Specific aspects of social support, such as having a spouse or adult child caregiver or having a caregiving relationship of at least three years' duration, moderated the impact of one type of stress (being highly dependent on others for care) on the risk of entering a nursing home.[7]

CASE EXAMPLE

Albert is a ten-year-old boy who suffers from cystic fibrosis. Albert's mother, Kate, is terrified of losing her son. Kate is very protective of Albert and will not allow him to go to school or even apply for the Make A Wish Foundation. Kate thinks if she protects Albert he will not die. Kate's overprotection of Albert is causing friction between her and her husband Gary. Gary thinks Albert should be allowed to do as he wishes within reason. Albert is becoming withdrawn and having more difficulty breathing. Dr. Gonzalez feels this is due to the stress that Albert is under. Albert has told Dr. Gonzalez he wishes he would die because then his parents would not fight anymore.

The Caregiver–Case Manager Relationship

In most cases the case manager will be welcomed gratefully into the household; he or she represents hope that assistance with respite care, personal care, transportation, financial obligations, legal services, and emotional support is at hand. It is not unusual for a caregiver to require a heavy amount of care in the first few months of service; the accumulation of strain, the unattended personal chores, and the need to feel like an independent person once again is critical. However, once a period of support has been delivered, many caregivers are ready to reassume more responsibility and the case manager can gradually reduce services.

There are some situations when the case manager will feel that the real client is the caregiver. The strain, the obligations, and the lack of a private life have so wounded the caregiver that the provision of formal services is of more benefit to the caregiver than to the client.

CASE EXAMPLE

Estelle was seventeen years old, although she looked much younger. She had assumed the role of primary caregiver for her mother, a woman in her late forties with crippling arthritis. Estelle's mother was totally incapacitated; her body was so twisted she could not sit, hold a cup, or even wipe her mouth.

Although Estelle had older sisters, they were all married with small children, leaving Estelle to provide care alone. Many days they would drop off their preschool children for her to babysit in addition to the demands of caring for her mother.

She had dropped out of school in the seventh grade, her teeth were badly rotted from a lack of dental care, she had never had a date, never been to a party or a shopping mall…she had missed her whole teenage years.

When the case manager made her first visit, she left in tears. Obviously, the mother was to be the recipient of the services but there was no doubt that the case manager's primary goal was to give Estelle back her life.

Not all caregiver–case manager interactions are pleasant. The caregiver may expect, even demand, much more care than the program is able to provide. She may criticize all the workers sent into the home for performing below her standards. She may resent losing the total dependence of the client.... All of these examples show how emotionally charged the caregiving role can be.

There will also be situations in which the caregiver holds that title in name only. The case manager will visit a home where the client is kept in a back room (or worse) and excluded from family activities. The dynamic of a family may have always been one of noncaring, the older person may be kept at home in order to control a Social Security check, the house may actually belong to the elder, or the family may have reached the point of burnout.

Rothman[8] lists reasons why a family is unable or unwilling to participate in caregiving. The client may have severe emotional problems, be relatively old, or have severe medical problems. There may also be other stress producers in the family which make additional responsibility overwhelming. They may be socially isolated or have other sources of emotional conflict.

EXERCISES

1. While performing your assessment, you catch the unmistakable smell of urine. What do you say?

2. When asked about her medical condition, the client tells you she has the "miseries." Where do you go from there?

3. Despite the fact that you have been working with a client for over a year, she still thinks you're Dorothy, her daughter-in-law. How do you handle it?

4. You know from experience that any visit to this client ends with her begging you to stay longer. Naturally, you feel guilty because you know how lonely she is. What can you do to alleviate this problem?

Discuss how you would handle these cases:

5. Two long-term rehabilitation patients have grown quite fond of each other. They come to you stating that they wish to live together and want you to find them an apartment. Both of these clients are in their early thirties. The man is a quadriplegic, and the woman is also a quadriplegic, but requires the use of a ventilator to live. The man has no family, however, the woman's parents are strongly opposed to these arrangements. There is a complex for the handicapped in town, and an apartment is available.

6. Wilma Jefferson is sixty-five years old. She suffered a stroke at the age of fifty-five that left her unable to speak and a quadriplegic. Her husband was also disabled from illness at the time of her stroke. Wilma was placed in a nursing home after the stroke as her only daughter was caring for Wilma's husband. Wilma's husband died the third year she was in the nursing home. After his death, the daughter brought Wilma to live with her.

Neither the daughter nor her husband work. The daughter's three sons have all had trouble with the legal system. Wilma began to suffer various infections and was in and out of the hospital. Wilma has stopped eating, and when she was asked if she knew she would die, she shook her head yes. Mrs. Jefferson was placed in the hospital, and a feeding tube was inserted. On her return home, Wilma cried frequently and would no longer interact with people. You have been brought in as the case manager and the daughter tells you that everything has to be done for her mother.

KEY TERMS

interviewing
defining needs
client–case manager relationships
caregivers

NOTES

1. Bissell, G. (1996). Personal ethics in social work with older people. *International Social Work, 39*, 257–263.
2. Ibid.
3. Robinson, K. M. (1997). The family's role in long-term care. *Journal of Gerontology Nursing, 23* (9), 7–11.
4. National Alliance for Caregiving and the American Association of Retired Persons. (1997). *Family caregiving in the U.S.—Findings from a national survey.*
5. Alzheimer's Association. (1991). *Time out! The case for a national family caregiver support policy.*
6. Feinberg, L. F. (1995). Private sorrows/public issues: The needs of family caregivers. *Journal of Mental Health and Aging, 1,* 213–219.
7. Pearlman, D. N., & Crown, W. H. (1992). Alternative sources of social support and their impacts on institutional risk. *The Gerontologist, 32*, 527–535.
8. Rothman, J. (1992). *Guidelines for case management: Putting research to professional use.* Itasca, IL: F. E. Peacock.

CHAPTER

8 Working with Other Agencies

One of the most difficult aspects of case management is the actual coordinating and monitoring of care—ensuring that services needed are obtained and delivered in a timely manner. **Interagency coordination** is a necessary ingredient in the delivery of human services and one of the most difficult to achieve. Agency autonomy is a precious and well-guarded commodity, creating a tension toward increasing self-sufficiency rather than sharing resources.[1] The players must have the capacity to cooperate, whether by controlling or significantly influencing required resources or the legal authority to enter into a joint venture. They must each exhibit a willingness to participate. Even under a legislative mandate, an agency that has either neutral or negative attitudes toward cooperation will be at the least an annoyance and at most a complete obstacle. Public awareness of the target population and its problems affect the ability of an organization to provide services. Having a client group that not only has clout in its own right but holds favorable public attention is a positive motivator for interagency coordination.[2]

Types of Interagency Projects

In some instances efficiencies in operation and program expansion can be achieved by dovetailing administrative operations among agencies. For example, information and referral services, case management, and a single point of access for services are designed to operate across agency lines.

Information Management

Information and referral (I&R) services are designed to offer the client population a single point of information on services. Ideally, the client or the family contacts the agency, outlines the problem, and the I&R agency provides a list of agencies providing that care. In some cases, the I&R agency initiates contact and follows up to make sure the provider agency at least made an effort to deliver services. Unfortunately, many agencies purporting to offer information and referral concentrate their efforts on their own services, thereby offering no expansion of information to the interested public.

Case Management

The other interagency management effort is case management. When the case management agency is performing in a brokerage role, it matches the needs of clients with the offerings of agencies. For a provider agency, either profit or nonprofit, that depends on clients for its income and existence, a strong dependent relationship is formed with the case management agency. This provides the case management agency with economic and political importance. Likewise, the case management agency must have a good working relationship with provider agencies—determining that a service is needed is useless if it cannot be located and arranged.

Types of Interagency Relationships

The case manager is often involved in two different types of interagency relationships: those agencies that contract for services to be provided under the authority of the case management system and those agencies that house programs with eligibility requirements allowing them to serve the same clients as the case management program.

The differences between the two affiliations is similar to the comparison of an organization that employs paid workers as well as utilizing volunteers. The compensated employees can be given a list of duties, disciplined if those duties are not performed correctly, and discharged if necessary. The volunteer workers, however, are requested to perform tasks with little or no control over the quality or quantity that they contribute. So, too, are the variations in working with agencies under contract and those that are not. While good management and human skills facilitate both relationships, the degree of control is strongly divergent.

Rothman[3] describes several types of authority that the case manager (through the agency) can have over other providers. *Administrative authority* is founded on policies and procedures from legal contracts or interagency agreements which clearly specify the right of the case manager to authorize, monitor, and terminate services. Whether such an arrangement is based on financial reimbursement or simply mandated by policy as with an umbrella agency, there is a clear line of control.

Legal authority is a legislative mandate that designates an organization responsible for a particular service or a particular population. Both child abuse and elder abuse fall into this category; reported cases must be investigated without hesitation or negotiation. Regulatory agencies responsible for the licensing of entities such as nursing homes, home health agencies, and child care centers also do not have a choice about which nursing homes will be inspected and which ones can be ignored. Likewise, the regulated industries owe their continuing operation to the actions of the regulatory ones, creating opportunities for coordination (both positive and negative).

Fiscal authority gives the case manager control over funding used to purchase services, either for an individual client, a caseload, or all the clients of an agency.

Fiscal authority can take several forms: the case manager can choose to buy services from among several providers, the case manager can refuse payment for insufficient or poor quality services, or the case manager can terminate the financial arrangement with one agency and initiate a new contract with another.

Joint funding authority creates a symbiotic relationship; two or more agencies are given resources to provide services under an interagency program. Each must uphold its obligation to the project, whether by contributing funds, personnel, or clients. Major programmatic decisions must be agreed upon, encouraging or even forcing cooperation. One agency that refuses to fulfill its role in a network may damage the program but it also places that organization at risk of losing the resources it needs from the others.

Other types of authority are less formal but can prove just as important. One is serving as a source of clients for the agency. Whether the clients provide the payment or the agency bills a third party (such as insurance or the government) for services provided, a human service agency without sufficient clients faces fiscal problems. The positioning of the case management agency as a major source of business for the provider agency creates an authority that may be informal but influential.

Another interagency relationship is the sharing of personnel. Having the services of qualified professional staff is necessary for any human service agency to operate. When the availability or cost of expertise is beyond an agency's capacity, arrangements with other agencies for joint staffing create a strong incentive for cooperation. Loaning personnel benefits both agencies: the original organization is relieved of the overhead cost while still being able to provide the service and the new organization supplements its staff. Sometimes the loaned worker performs as a regular staff member of the new agency while being paid by the original one. In other situations, called out-stationing, the worker is still supervised by the original agency but operates out of another office due to convenience to clients or project managers, or access to technical resources. Clearly, such arrangements create or reinforce interagency activities; they may also create or reinforce turf issues.

Interagency coordination can be judged by three elements: comprehensiveness, compatibility, and cooperation. *Comprehensiveness* refers to the extent to which all the necessary ingredients for a successful implementation are present in the system. *Compatibility* describes the ability of the different parts to operate together and *cooperation* refers to the extent they actually do work together.[4]

Working with Noncontract Agencies

A primary function of a case manager is to link clients with all resources for which they are eligible. This involves not only the services offered by the parent agency, but also the other programs in the community sponsored by social service, health care, business, and financial institutions. Few clients can be appropriately served through just one agency.

TABLE 8.1   Possible Service Providers for One Client

Mr. Perkins is receiving	from
Case management	Case management agency
Homemaker service	Case management agency
Personal care	Public health department
Subsidized rent	Housing authority
Food stamps	Welfare office
Home-delivered meal	Area agency on aging
Friendly visiting	Church
Emergency response system	County hospital
Financial counseling	Bank
Legal assistance	Area agency on aging
SSI	Social Security office
Medical insurance	Medicaid
Medical care	Physician

The example in Table 8.1 is not extreme; many persons receiving assistance under a case management system will indeed be affiliated with many other agencies. Mr. Perkins receives services from only one agency, the homemaker agency, over which the case manager has any control. Yet, whatever problem arises in any service, Mr. Perkins will seek assistance from the case manager.

The relationship also works in the other direction. Any one of the involved agencies could have been the referral source for case management; the organization attempting to serve him could not provide the necessary assistance alone and turned to the case management agency to supplement what care they were providing. What exists in the community is a network of agencies that are interdependent on each other for the provision of a complete package of services.

Agencies are said to be interdependent if they must take each other into account to accomplish their individual goals. Given the environment of increasingly scarce resources in the social services, this alliance has become essential to the success of any one program. What evolves is a negotiation of services: I'll provide for yours if you provide for mine.

Knowing Providers

It is important not only to know who the providers are, but what they do. Many agencies keep extensive databases of outside resources; some are more accurate and up-to-date than others. The case manager can operate more efficiently by maintaining an accurate database of each provider's services, requirements, intake procedures, and objectives. Making it a practice to revise the information each time there is a change in the provider's operation keeps the information current, to both the case manager's and the client's advantage. Social and health services organizations are often affected by economic, policy, or personnel changes; how these reorganizations affect service delivery is essential information for finding and securing services for clients.

Case managers have found that identifying one or two people at a provider agency who seem to be helpful can be of great benefit. By establishing a good professional relationship and making contact on a regular basis, the case manager has a better chance of getting phone calls returned, clients enrolled, and valid referrals. The common concerns for the client can make it easier to see each other as allies and to better understand what to expect and what not to expect.

Sometimes subtle differences can decide whether or not a provider will accept a client. Case managers, in one sense, are marketing their client to the outside provider—selling them as clients the provider can and should serve. Knowing the outcomes that are important to the provider (for instance, an adult education program interested in increasing the number of regular students), and offering the client in that aspect (this client has had excellent attendance at the rehabilitation center), makes the client more attractive. This will provide the agency with a rationale for accepting the client for service.

It is also essential that the client understand the provider. Each delivery system expects certain behaviors from those using it; educating the client ahead of time will prevent problems later on. Information on fees, consequences of tardiness or absences, and documents that must be provided should all be explained.

Establishing an Interagency Relationship

Several devices can be employed to promote interagency cooperation. The most effective of these is to enter into a contract for the delivery of services. By both agencies agreeing in detail to what will be provided, to whom, and under whose direction, a procedure for scheduling of service is put into place. Often, the road to a contract starts out with less formal contacts.

Because there is an obvious overlap in organizational interests, indicated by the possibility of sharing clients, coordinating agencies should begin to develop a relationship. This may begin as an informal agreement and evolve into a formal contract. The first step is to decide what types of projects, clients, or services could be shared. Next, the two agencies should identify the internal personnel who are not only willing to establish a cooperative relationship but have the authority to do so. Never diminishing the value of a friendly voice at another agency who can assist with information or suggestions, the best relationships are those that are dependable and enforceable.

Having a strong idea of what the other agency has done in the past, where their funding comes from, who the leadership is within the agency, what past associations have worked well and which were problematic will place the negotiating case manager in a strong position. Once the relationship has been established, the agencies can provide each other with policy and procedure manuals, copies of their intake forms, lists of which employees to contact for varying needs, and other information that will make the association easier. Having such knowledge makes referrals more accurate and prevents wasting the time of both organizations. It is important to maintain an interagency liaison's health through regular communication. A regular exchange of forms or email, periodic case conferences, shared training, and even an interoffice luncheon will strengthen the association.

Formalized letters of agreement are also used to establish guidelines for interagency referrals and shared services. While not as binding as a contract, they delineate the expectations of each party and give the case managers more confidence that needed services will be provided to their clients.

Who's in Charge?

When scheduling a standard service from another agency for a client, the case manager is indicating a willingness to take responsibility for coordination. This arrangement is satisfactory to most agencies because it relieves them from a great deal of the obligation of care provision; they are pleased to know whom to call if a client is having difficulties. The challenge is to ensure cooperation without threatening the autonomy of the other agency. Seen from the other side, the process of scheduling resources for a client is a request for money, staff time, and effort. The service provider must gain something from the transaction, whether it is increased funding, higher visibility, or a promise of cooperation in the future. They may also feel a loss; services provided to your client cannot be delivered to another, and they experience a loss of control over the success or failure of a project. The case manager who keeps these points in mind can more effectively negotiate services.

Requesting a different service or a waiver of eligibility requirements will produce a very cool reception. It seems to be a fact of bureaucracy that the larger the agency, the more services it can give and the more rules it has for giving (or not giving) services. The case manager will undoubtedly encounter situations in which the client is only slightly ineligible for a service that they desperately need. When approached by the case manager to modify the requirements, the outside agency will not welcome the disruption of their routine operation.

Before the case manager makes the initial contact with a new agency, it would be wise to do some investigation into the history of the relationship between the two organizations. Knowing what occurred can help forewarn of and possibly avoid difficulty before the case manager becomes personally involved. Even if the case management system is new, it is likely that the parent agency has past dealings with the group with which the case manager is now working. Any past conflicts among agencies and professional groups or between individual service providers must be anticipated.

The key to successful interagency relationships is to continually increase the scope of influence. By supplying relevant information, keeping promises, offering assistance to other agencies, and giving recognition for cooperation, a favorable professional reputation will encourage teamwork.

Monitoring Services of Other Agencies

Unfortunately, a case manager will be involved in cases where the services are not delivered appropriately or at all. Sometimes there is a true lack of resources, sometimes there is a misunderstanding of what is expected, and sometimes the other agency will simply refuse. Monitoring of these agencies can be very complicated. Many outside agencies consider that they are contributing services to someone else's client and that the agency with primary responsibility should be satisfied with what they get. Case managers fear that too many complaints will result in a termination of assistance altogether.

One manner of preventing conflict is to provide updates on clients as a regular feature, relating the successes as well as the failures. The cooperating agency will be more likely to seriously address complaints if they understand that the case manager is an unbiased monitor.

Monitoring Requirements

Many times the case management agency is involved with providers that are regulated by governmental agencies, either because of the type of service (such as a nursing home) or because of the payment source (such as Title XX). Whether the regulations are established on the federal, state, local level, or a combination of these, often the case management agency is charged by their sponsoring source to verify that the provider agencies are legally qualified to provide services.

For example, home health agencies providing service financed by the Medicare program must meet Medicare's conditions of participation, which include requirements addressing patients' rights; compliance with federal, state, and local laws; mandated organizational and administrative structures; standards of training and qualifications for personnel; and establishment of a professional advisory group. Agencies and individuals providing service financed under Medicaid must also meet training and qualification requirements.[5] State-funded programs in mental health, juvenile justice, protective services, nursing home care and rehabilitation will all be under a mixture of federal and state requirements.

Advocacy

One of the first and saddest lessons the case manager learns is that no matter how skillful he or she may be, if the services are not present, case management skills are of little use. Advocacy comes into play only when connecting and negotiation alone are unable to provide the necessary fit between the client's concerns and usable resources. Connecting relies on accurate information and clear communication. Negotiation adds the dimensions of trust building and creating mutually acceptable alternatives. For successful advocacy, it is often necessary to bring in the element of power.

Two types of advocacy are important: that which takes place at the individual patient level and that at the systems level. Perhaps the most frequently occurring situation that requires advocacy on an individual level is when patients must overcome barriers that keep them from getting the services or entitlements they need. This includes situations in which a patient has difficulty getting linked to a service and situations in which a patient is being dropped from a service.

Many times such problems can be overcome by the case manager through informal interpersonal negotiations. However, in more difficult cases it may be necessary for case managers to enlist the support of supervisory or administrative staff members within their own agency or even to make use of more formal channels. This may involve seeking the assistance of legal aid services or traditional advocacy groups.

Advocacy on a systems level is a somewhat different case management function. In general, it involves someone taking responsibility for calling attention to some service system deficiency that adversely affects a large number or class of clients. Systems level advocacy often requires political action and is especially appropriate for citizens groups.[6]

In the process of linking clients with available community resources, it is sometimes necessary for the case manager to overcome barriers to the receipt of services. A client may be denied services because of eligibility requirements or restrictive regulations. Others may be less formally rejected through the inadequate or infrequent provision of services to which they are entitled.

In the capacity of advocate, a case manager will present complaints, appeals, or requests to the service agency. The ability to successfully negotiate on behalf of the client depends in large part on the relationships the case manager develops with the other agencies. In many cases a good informal relationship can accomplish much more than a formal appeal. Sometimes a worker at a bureaucratic organization will be frustrated with the lengthy eligibility procedures and will either instruct the case manager on ways to speed the process or handle the matter themselves.

When a personal contact is ineffective, it then becomes necessary for the case manager to involve his supervisor and, as a result, his agency in the advocacy process. A formal request from the director of one agency to another carries a higher degree of demand as well as documentation of the request.

Occasionally, a case manager will realize that the problems with a client and another agency are not isolated but only an example of similar situations. When the case manager determines that another agency is inadequately serving a portion or all of the client population, the case manager's supervisor should be notified so that class advocacy can be considered.

Ballew and Mink[7] suggest five escalating levels of advocacy.

1. *Make a direct appeal for a denied resource.* Many times simply interceding on a client's behalf with another agency will accomplish the objective. There may have been erroneous communication; the provider may not have understood the

request or the client may not have understood the process. By contacting a counterpart at the provider agency and detailing what is needed, what steps have been taken so far, and the response the client received, the provider should be able to explain the difficulty.

If the situation was not caused by an obvious provider error, the case manager can try to make the client's case, explaining the need and why the provider is the proper one to meet that need. The more professional and nonconfrontational the case manager's demeanor is at this point, the more likely an agreement will be reached. Obviously, the more known about the policies and procedures of helping organizations, both formal and informal, the better an advocate the case manager can be. Pointing out policy in an unaccusing manner may get the point across.

2. *Appeal to higher authority.* The next step is to take the matter to the supervisory level. Organizational norms usually specify that the case manager goes to her own superior, rather than confronting the provider supervisor. It is quite possible that these two have dealt with each other on other matters and may have established a working relationship for solving such issues.

3. *Use a grievance process.* Most larger private and all government agencies that deal in the distribution of benefits are required to have an internal procedure for administrative hearings. A case manager who works with a particular agency on a regular basis, especially one that seems to fall short of expectations, should have information on the appeals process. Making denied clients aware of the process, connecting them with legal assistance, or actually filing a grievance on their behalf are all options.

4. *Appeal to outside authority.* Many of the providers in the health and social fields are regulated or funded by federal, state, or local agencies. If the basis for denying the client falls into an area covered by these regulations, a written appeal may be submitted asking for intervention.

5. *Legal action.* The final step that can be made as an advocate is to assist the client in legal action, usually through a civil suit.

Obviously, as each step becomes more confrontational and can have harsher implications for the provider agency, the case manager becomes more likely to alienate the agency. At each point an evaluation must be made whether the gains possible are sufficient to jeopardize a future working relationship and possible assistance for other clients. The safest course of action for a case manager is to defer decisions of this weight to the administration of the agency.

Working with Contract Agencies

The case manager has a different connection with an agency that is providing services under a contract. Hopefully, the document will have specified the types of services, the quality of services, and will have given the case manager or someone else at the agency the authority to schedule and evaluate the contracting agency's performance.

Monitoring Services

Most case management systems assign all or part of the monitoring activities to the case managers. Formal methods of evaluation are used on a regular basis while an informal appraisal is a constant exercise. The primary assessment to be performed is the assurance that services are being delivered in the quantity and with the quality for which they have contracted. Quantity, the type and amount of a service, can be traced through time sheets and billings; it is an objective procedure. Rating quality, however, creates the necessity of value judgments on tasks that the case manager may not be qualified to grade. Assessing the nutritional value of meals, the manner in which a client is given a bath, or an injection of medication is not within the field of knowledge of the average case manager.

If the agency does not have an existing method of officially judging the quality of services, the case manager can request assistance from other persons within the agency or from persons outside the agency who possess the necessary qualifications. Beyond this, the case manager must rely on the reports of clients, families, physicians, other service providers, as well as the case manager's observations to informally assess the quality of care. Usually these reports will come in the form of complaints which require an investigation and resolution.

Client Satisfaction

Community services have always considered client satisfaction to be a strong indicator of quality. One study looked at the qualities that recipients of personal care services cited as being the most desirable. These included:

1. workers' arrival on scheduled days, time, and working for the scheduled amount of time;
2. completion of work with consistency;
3. neat and clean appearance;
4. care for and protection of the customer's safety and property;
5. honesty, trustworthiness, courtesy, and respect;
6. responsiveness to the customer's preferences; and
7. empathetic and cheerful demeanor.[8]

Problem Resolution

The provision of in-home services under a case management system involves a minimum of three parties: the case manager, the client, and the provider. Difficulties can come from any of the three sources and between all combinations of those involved.

Client versus Provider

The client complains that the service provider:

1. does not come on time;
2. does not perform what the client expects;
3. does not remain in the home long enough;
4. does not perform as well as the client expects;
5. is not friendly or courteous;
6. becomes personally involved in family matters.

Provider versus Case Manager

The provider may approach the program supervisor stating that the case manager:

1. expects unreasonable tasks;
2. ignores the provider's suggestions;
3. has scheduled inappropriate care;
4. has misapplied policy;
5. tries to directly supervise workers outside the chain of command.

Provider versus Client

The provider will relate to the case manager that the client or the family:

1. is uncooperative;
2. harasses the workers;
3. expects more work than has been agreed upon;
4. is not at home when workers arrive.

An overall examination of these complaints leads to the conclusion that a careful delineation of the rights and responsibilities of each party *before* care provision is initiated will prevent later problems.

Working with Other Professionals

In addition to the organizational structures with which a case manager must deal, he is also in a position to personally interact with professionals in other agencies and other disciplines. The differences in backgrounds, priorities, and approaches can create conflict, even when each party considers itself to be performing in the best interest of the client. It is imperative that case managers understand the value of a cooperative relationship.

It is the differences among professional ideologies that seem to be the source of many interagency and interprofessional conflicts. Thus, the case manager must be able to work cooperatively with diverse professional groups with conflicting ideas and ideals.

Potential Professional Conflicts

The Physician

Very few case management systems operate without requiring input and cooperation from the client's physician, creating the necessity of a comfortable relationship. However, many case managers have expressed that the problems encountered in this area generate more frustration than any other. Physicians will refuse to complete or sign forms authorizing care, will incorrectly complete forms which delays the delivery of services, or will expect more of a case management system than can be provided. Some will not complete forms unless they receive payment, which is prohibited under many government programs.

Experienced case managers have developed several means of improving their contacts with physicians. Many medical offices are actually run by a nurse or office manager. By soliciting this person's support, the case manager can often accomplish needed activities. Some case managers have asked to make a presentation to the local medical society in order to explain the benefits of the program to the client and to the physician. In cases that the physician cannot be convinced to work with the case manager, the family has been asked to intercede and solicit cooperation. As a last resort, the case manager may inform the client that, due to the failure of the physician to provide necessary verification, the client is advised to seek alternate medical care.

The Nurse

Most encounters between nurses and case managers take place in the clients' homes. Usually the nurse is affiliated with another program that is used to complement the case management services.

Conflict can arise when one professional does not agree with the type or amount of care the other is providing; either they are considered to be encouraging dependency with too many services or risking the safety of the client with too few. If the two programs are officially coordinated in any way, a conference with supervisors, and the client if possible, may allow for an airing of differences and a compromise. If there is no official association, it may be sufficient to realize the different orientations of the two disciplines and accept them gracefully.

The Hospital Social Worker

The growth of case management programs has been received by hospital discharge planners in two opposite ways: They love it or they hate it. Many see this system, which operates in the community, as a blessed resource to which clients can be referred, relieving them of the responsibility of making outside arrangements and conducting follow-up evaluations. Others feel that this program is an encroachment on their field. This attitude is heightened by the fact that most hospital social workers possess higher degrees and licenses than does the average case manager.

Interorganizational relationships are strongest as the degree of dependence of one organization on another increases. An array of structural factors such as size, resources, and complexity are determinates of interorganizational relations. An organization wishing to improve its case management in relation to external support agencies can do so by providing appropriate incentives, including use of intrusive means of influence. Interorganizational relationships are facilitated when there is mutual dependency and an exchange of resources among participating agencies. As the degree of dependency of an organization on another increases, the dependent agency becomes vulnerable to the demands of the other organization and less able to implement its own policies. This may block creativity and innovation, but it may also ensure access to needed resources. Interorganizational relationships are not stable but change with time, particularly as the size, sophistication, and experience of an agency increases.[9]

EXERCISES

1. The homemaker complains to you that the family members expect him to clean up after all of them. They demand that he wash their dishes, clean their rooms, and do all of their laundry. What do you do?

2. Your client was also receiving services from Agency X, but they have suddenly terminated him. You think there has been an error. What do you do?

3. A family member has called your supervisor and complained about something you did or said. You must now go back into the home knowing they will be there. What do you say?

4. If you don't get the medical forms signed by the client's physician by tomorrow, the case will terminate. The receptionist keeps telling you that the forms will be sent but they are not. How do you get the forms signed?

KEY TERMS

interagency
coordination
supervision

NOTES

1. Austin, C. (1993). Case management: A systems perspective. *Families in society, 74*(8), 451–459.
2. Merrit, J., & Neugeboren, B. (1990). Factors affecting agency capacity for inter-organizational coordination. *Administration in Social Work, 14* (4), 73–85.

3. Rothman, J. (1992). *Guidelines for case management: Putting research to professional use.* Itasca, IL: F. E. Peacock.

4. Austin, C. (1993). Case management: a systems perspective. *Families in society, 74*(8), 451–459.

5. General Accounting Office. *Long-term care: Status of quality assurance and measurement in home and community-based services* (Letter Report, 03/31/94, GAO/PEMD-94-19).

6. Intagliata, J., Willer, B., & Egri, G. (1988). The role of the family in delivering case management services. In M. Harris and L. Bachrach (Eds.), *Clinical case management.* San Francisco: Jossey-Bass.

7. Ballew, J., & Mink, G. (1996). *Case management in social work.* Springfield, IL: Charles C. Thomas.

8. General Accounting Office. *Long-term care: Status of quality assurance and measurement in home and community-based services* (Letter Report, 03/31/94, GAO/PEMD-94-19).

9. Rothman, J. (1992). *Guidelines for case management: Putting research to professional use.* Itasca, IL: F. E. Peacock.

CHAPTER

9

Case Management as a Profession

Case management as a separate and legitimate profession is still evolving. Undoubtedly, the obstacle to the professionalization of the role is the varied models, standards, definitions, tasks, and personnel associated with the title. As long as one agency requires masters-level social workers and another agency down the street uses volunteers without any requirements or training, there will be problems. Similarly, while Agency A case managers act as advocates to obtain full services for their clients and Company B case managers are responsible for limiting services under a cost cap, there will be problems.

Characteristics of Case Managers

Some research has been performed on case managers themselves: Who are they and what do they do? What makes a "good" case manager? What personality traits do they share?

Personality Traits

A study by Quick[1] examined the personality traits of case managers. The case managers in the sample population rated agreeableness as their strongest personality trait, followed by intellect, conscientiousness, extroversion, and emotionality. Persons who are *agreeable* are described as genuinely concerned with other people and try to treat everyone with courtesy and kindness; are quick to forgive; are cooperative and helpful; tend to be humble and modest; trust others and are generous, good-natured, soft hearted, and lenient. These qualities are important for case managers because they work with a variety of persons—physicians, clients, payers, and so on—who may exhibit contrary, inflexible, or demanding personalities that make them challenging to work with (see Table 9.1). Case managers must maintain a courteous and caring demeanor even in stressful situations. Persons lacking this trait would not be satisfied with the role of case manager due to the strong need for these qualities in this role.

The high scores for *intellect* indicate that case managers typically strive to learn and maintain current knowledge, which is essential in the health care field.

TABLE 9.1   Characteristics of Case Managers

Trait	Mean	Median	Mode	SD
Agreeableness	4.31	4	4	.72
Intellect	4.25	4	4	.68
Conscientiousness	4.23	4	4	.72
Extroversion	4.00	2	2	1.17
Emotionality	2.92	2	2	1.17

Quick, B. (1997). The relationship between personality traits and job satisfaction for case managers. *The Journal of Care Management, 3* (5): 78–82.

They must also be culturally sensitive, as their clients' cultural beliefs often affect their care. Creativity is required in finding the right treatment modality for each client based on the client's medical needs, lifestyle, and insurance benefits.

Conscientiousness is defined as being careful and hardworking. Case managers with this trait work toward their goals in a deliberate manner, have a relatively high need for achievement, are well organized, reliable, have good self-discipline, and take their obligations seriously. This trait is essential for case managers as many work very independently and carry heavy caseloads. They must be well organized in order to accomplish their goals.

Extroversion means sociable, gregarious, talkative, assertive, and active. Case managers require these qualities because interaction with others is a significant portion of their job. *Emotionality* means being prone to episodes of psychological distress, moody, overly sensitive, and dissatisfied with many aspects of their lives. This is essential for case managers as they deal with many types of persons, some with terminal illnesses. In addition, they find themselves in stressful situations, such as telling clients that their insurance benefits will not cover the medical care they need.

Another study by Nufer[2] had consumers and case managers to judge eighteen items on their importance for good case management. Interestingly enough, all eighteen were judged to be vital. Case managers are expected to provide timely, comprehensive, adequate services consistent with the desires of the consumers, and do so with enthusiasm and motivation in a thoughtful and respectful manner.

Case Manager Certification

There is much debate on the need for case manager certification. Those promoting the idea argue that, like other professions, case managers have an accepted body of knowledge and skills that indicate their ability to perform acceptably. It is also thought that standardizing the title of case manager will raise the status of the role in the professional community. Those opposed to certification point out that most case managers are trained as either social workers or nurses, both of which have their own licensure and certification process.

An independent agency, Certification of Insurance Rehabilitation Specialists Commission, has developed and administers a certification exam. As you have learned in this book, much of what case managers do is difficult to describe, let alone measure. To arrive at a body of core knowledge, the International Case Management Association and the CIRSC considered many official definitions of case management and conducted a nationwide survey to identify content for the examination requirements and levels for passing the examination. The certification can be renewed at five-year intervals if the individual demonstrates ongoing professional development through reexamination or an approved program of continuing education.[3]

Case Management Standards

State and local agencies along with other organizations such as the National Council on Aging and the National Association of Social Workers have established a number of case management standards. These **standards** typically address the core functions of the case management process, caseload size, and case manager qualifications. However, these standards often vary in specifics such as what a care plan should cover, what constitutes a reasonable caseload size, and what level and type of education case managers should have.

The standards published by NASW are quite detailed but cover ten basic concepts:

1. "The social work case manager shall have a baccalaureate or graduate degree from a social work program accredited by the Council on Social Work Education and shall possess the knowledge, skills, and experience necessary to competently perform case management activities."
2. "The social work case manager shall use his or her professional skills and competence to serve the client whose interests are of primary concern."
3. "The social work case manager shall ensure that clients are involved in all phases of case management practice to the greatest extent possible."
4. "The social work case manager shall ensure the client's right to privacy and ensure appropriate confidentiality when information about the client is released to others."
5. "The social work case manager shall intervene at the client level to provide and/or coordinate the delivery of direct services to clients and their families."
6. "The social work case manager shall intervene at the service systems level to support existing case management services and to expand the supply of and improve access to needed services."
7. "The social work case manager shall be knowledgeable about resource availability, service costs, and budgetary parameters and be fiscally responsible in carrying out all case management functions and activities. "

8. "The social work case manager shall participate in evaluative and quality assurance activities designed to monitor the appropriateness and effectiveness of both the service delivery system in which case management operates as well as the case manager's own case management services, and to otherwise ensure full professional accountability."

9. "The social work case manager shall carry a reasonable caseload that allows the case manager to effectively plan, provide, and evaluate case management tasks related to client and system interventions."

10. "The social work case manager shall treat colleagues with courtesy and respect and strive to enhance interprofessional, intraprofessional, and interagency cooperation on behalf of the client."[4]

An Assessment

A study by the General Accounting Office[5] found that all programs in its survey required a common assessment form when conducting a comprehensive needs assessment. The assessment forms typically address six main topics: medical needs, function capacity, cognitive abilities, safety and environmental considerations, financial situation, and social needs. It is also standard that a home visit is required during the assessment process. Having a standardized form ensures that sufficient and relevant information is collected and assures equitable access into the program. Some programs set time limits between the time of the referral and the initiation and/or completion of the assessment.

A Care Plan

Case managers are also expected to obtain input from clients and, whenever possible, their families and service providers when developing a care plan. There is normally a time limitation on the completion of the care plan.

The standards for the purchase and arranging of services vary. Sometimes limitations are set on the cost of the entire caseload, allowing more flexibility in arranging services for clients whose needs exceed the average for a short period of time. Others set limitations, either a dollar amount or an hour amount, for each client, monthly or annually. Still others do not purchase services at all, simply referring clients to service agencies.

Client–Case Manager Interaction

Standards also vary on the required contacts during a case. Usually requirements specify the frequency, generally at least a monthly telephone contact and face-to-face less frequently. Some, however, require a face-to-face each month. All the state programs that were reviewed by the National Association of State Units on Aging (NASUA) require that a case manager conduct at least some in-home visits. NASUA reports that, in 75 percent of these programs, case managers are required to contact clients, at least by phone, within three-month intervals. The remaining states require such contact at six-month intervals. There have been no evaluations to determine why these intervals were chosen or if there is a difference in the effectiveness or efficiency of care.[6] A reassessment process requiring a new assessment to be completed can range from every six months to every twelve months. It is not uncommon for case managers to be in more frequent contact with their clients, particularly during periods of instability or crisis.

Caseload Size

Often a program will determine the optimal caseload size per case manager; often these are recommendations rather than regulations, and often these decisions are made as guesses rather than based on any real evidence on the appropriate number. Even when there is policy stating the caseload size, it is usually given as an average or a target. Affected by financial and managerial restraints, the administration often must be able to increase caseloads during drops in the budget, a shortness of personnel, or a lack of office space. Although most case managers stated that a limit on the number of cases that could be assigned to them was necessary to maintain the quality of case management services, they did not agree on what the standard should be, even within agencies.[7]

Case Management Associations

As the profession of case management has developed, its members have begun to organize into professional associations. As with most interdisciplinary roles, different groups focus on different aspects of the case manager role.

Case Management Society of America

Founded in 1990, the Case Management Society of America (CMSA) is an international, nonprofit, professional organization serving the case management marketplace. Its mission is to promote individual and collective professional development of health care case management services. CMSA reports over 7,500 members and more than 150 developing and affiliated chapters, including international locations.

CMSA defines case management as a collaborative process that assesses, plans, implements, coordinates, monitors, and evaluates options and services to meet an individual's health needs through communications and available resources to promote quality, cost-effective outcomes. In 1995, CMSA published *The Standards of Practice for Case Management*. These standards provide the guideline for practice excellence.

CMSA, in 1996, developed the Center for Case Management Accountability (CCMA®)—an outcomes initiative which is creating the framework for case management accountability, defining case management outcomes, and developing a mechanism for reporting and comparing performance measurements on a national basis. The purpose of CCMA is to provide a mechanism for the measurement, evaluation, and reporting of case management outcomes. Its goals are to provide a framework for measuring accountability by providing the methodology for data collection and documentation of results and thus demonstrating value, to establish a standard for assessing the value of case management, and finally, to provide the information necessary to identify best practice and thereby improve the delivery of case management services. The *Journal of Care Management* is CMSA's official journal.

National Association of Social Work

The National Association of Social Work (NASW) created standards for social work case management, stating that it recognizes that there is no universally accepted definition of case management nor is there one definitive model of case management as practiced within the social work profession. However, the NASW has yet to create a formal subdivision of case management or to endorse an affiliated organization for that purpose.

Case Management Ethics

The need for a solid understanding of **ethics** is an important issue for case managers. The act of assuming decision-making power over the life and quality of life of another person is a serious responsibility; a case manager must have internal as well as organizational guidance. Abramson (1996) defines ethical decision making as "taking a rational, impartial, impersonal perspective in order to analyze problems according to ethical principles, prioritize possible actions and principles and select a resolution that fits with the most important principles."[8]

Serving the Client Well

Many times ethical behavior is simply considerate behavior. For a case manager, putting the client's needs above the agency's, above the payer's, and sometimes above the case manager's own expression keeps the interest of the client as the primary concern. Several processes are available to case managers when faced with decisions that affect the care, and therefore the well-being, of the client.

The case manager should ask the advice of colleagues and supervisors whenever such consultation is in the best interests of the clients. Many agencies have weekly consulting sessions, either each case manager with the supervisor, the case managers as a group, or sessions based around individual clients with only those involved in the case attending. Often others will have encountered similar problems and can offer their experience. Further, if the situation is serious, a decision by the case manager may impact financially, ethically, or legally on the agency, making notification of the supervisory staff mandatory.

Case managers should select the types, amounts, and providers of services that best address the client's needs. Pressure from agencies to decrease care for financial reasons, increase care to maximize hours of other in-house workers, or schedule workers with a history of client conflict may place the case manager in a difficult position. If pressures are from external agencies with which the case manager's agency contracts, the supervisory staff needs to be notified. Unfortunately, some case managers are employed by agencies that also offer the services the case manager is authorized to schedule. It may be difficult to adhere to a position of primacy of the client's interests, particularly in a climate of resource scarcity. Agency cost containment goals may conflict with the best interests of the client. In these cases, asking for written agency policy on the handling of differences of opinion will at least give the case manager a sense of their latitude. When primacy of the client's interest runs counter to agency goals, policies, or resources and ethical dilemmas are encountered, peer review or ethics committees are needed.

A case manager also has the obligation to terminate a service when it is no longer needed by or no longer helpful to the client. Many times this is not supported by the client or the family; they have come to rely on the services. If, however, the case manager believes that the client is no longer eligible due to an improvement or deterioration in condition, a change in financial status, residency, or any other qualification, it is an action that must be taken.

CASE EXAMPLE

Mr. Cannon had been a client for over a year following a hip fracture. His surgery and physical therapy had progressed well and it was recommended by the physician that home services be terminated. Grace, the case manager, knew how much Mr. Cannon depended on the homemaker she had placed in the home, as much for company as for the cooking and cleaning. Upon learning that the case would close, Mr. Cannon pleaded with Grace to keep the case open and even claimed to be having assorted pains that would make his case eligible once again.

Grace's first impulse was sympathy for this pleasant man with whom she had developed a friendship. However, in discussing the dilemma with her supervisor, she realized that his isolation was self-imposed and as long as companionship was being provided by the homemaker, he had no incentive to find other social outlets.

Autonomy

Client **autonomy** is a fundamental value in the case management process. As discussed in Chapter 1, case managers must be committed to the principles of client empowerment and participation, as well as to the ultimate goal of the process—that clients become able to manage themselves. Clients are to be involved in the process as much as possible, and treatment plans must support client choice and promote self-sufficiency. At the same time, the case manager has the obligation to provide the client with quality services and to act in his or her best interests.

Sometimes, the case manager may believe that what the client prefers is not in his or her interest; this situation can entail an ethical conflict.

In an effort to encourage client participation, case managers can regard autonomy in a broader sense than just giving the individual the right to make choices. Positive autonomy means that the case manager works to broaden and strengthen the autonomy that the client has. If client preferences will result in danger to the client or others, the case manager must find a way to make those preferences more appropriate.

There are several instances in which client autonomy is not an absolute priority: for example, when client preferences interfere with other clients or other helping professionals, when the client is not competent to make decisions, and when clients need protection from their own decisions. In such situations, the case manager must have a clear conception of the reasons why autonomy should be restricted.

Confidentiality

Confidentiality requires that members of a group trusted with personal physical, emotional, mental, financial, and social information of a client, do not reveal any of that information to outsiders. Information may be shared with professional caregivers if permission is granted such as when applying for services for a client, filing a complaint on behalf of a client, or obtaining information to determine eligibility. However, it is never appropriate to discuss cases with the general public. In those professional situations such as trainings, conferences, or planning committees, a case manager may discuss the elements of a case in order to illustrate a point or ask for suggestions but no identifying information should be revealed. One should also limit the discussion to valid reasons for imparting information; telling cute or tragic stories about clients around the office creates an atmosphere not flattering to the dignity or privacy of the client population.

This issue comes up often when the case manager receives a written or verbal request from another agency or private individual. At these times, these factors should be considered:

1. No information should be released without the informed consent of the client or the client's legal representative. *Informed consent* is defined as awareness of what information is being released, the purpose of the release, and the identity of the recipient. On the chance that the client or caregiver could deny having given permission or understanding why or to whom it was being released, a written statement should be prepared which not only states that permission is being allowed but outlines the reason for the request. Having such a document signed will prevent later problems.

2. Only the minimum information required should be released, and only to the appropriate entity. Sometimes case managers, feeling a kinship with others in the social welfare or health care field, are glad to share what they know about a mutual client. However, going beyond the implication of the question and volunteering other information not only may influence the care the client receives but also may color the attitude of the other worker.

CASE EXAMPLE

Sharon, the case manager, really enjoyed her client, Stephie. She had worked with Stephie through her pregnancy and was now proud to have helped her obtain her first real job. So when Sharon got a call from the food stamp office worker to verify Stephie's social security number, Sharon told the worker about how well Stephie was doing. The food stamp worker was interested, indeed, because Stephie had not reported any earned income and began a fraud investigation.

---

3. Recipients of information must be informed that the information is confidential and may not be passed any further without additional consent of the client. Regardless of the attention paid to confidentiality in one agency, the professionally justified sharing of it with another opens up many more possibilities for inappropriate disclosure. It would be preferred to send each shared bit of information in writing, along with a warning of confidentiality. This, however, is not always possible since much information is exchanged over the phone or through electronic mail. For these cases, the originating agency can best protect itself and its clients by developing interagency agreements, periodically reviewed and renewed, that state the assumption of confidentiality in exchanged information.

4. Be aware that communications between a client and a case manager are not considered privileged by legal authority. First, the case manager is warned that all client information is secret, then they learn that it is not legally protected. Unlike other professionals who deal with personal issues of the public, social workers (and therefore case managers) have no sacred oath of silence. If information on a client is needed by a legal authority, the officer of the court should be encouraged to obtain a subpoena to protect the agency from further civil actions. Case managers may be required to testify in court and must do so.

5. The case manager is bound by the decision of the client or the client's representative as to the release of information. Here, once again, the element of client choice appears. There may be times when the case manager feels it would be in the client's best interest to share information (to qualify for additional benefits) or to refuse to divulge information (credit companies). A case manager may advise the client but the client's determination is final.

6. A client has the right of access to information contained in the client's file. Very rarely does a client actually request to read his file, yet the case manager must always be aware that the possibility exists. Beyond any other considerations of professional behavior, the recognition that characterizations, descriptions, unprofessional remarks, or unsubstantiated statements could someday be shown to the client or a legal representative should motivate case managers to use discretion and restraint. This may be an effort with some more difficult clients but well worth the trouble avoided.

Electronic Confidentiality

An issue in confidentiality that must be considered is the input of client information in data management systems and the possibility of information retrieved by unauthorized persons. These systems are established on the administrative level to collect demographic information, to justify expenditures, to provide a means for billing for services, or provide a basis for research. Some systems carry only billing information; these, however, are a source for names, social security numbers, Medicaid numbers, and types of services offered. Software used for client tracking may contain medical diagnosis, mental state, income, names of family members, and other private information. Unfortunately, most clients accepting assistance from agencies are not aware that information gathered at the assessment becomes computer entries.

The last few years have brought increased concern over electronic records, particularly those accessible through the Internet. It should be noted, however, that as the availability of client information through technology has increased, so have the methods for maintaining its security. However, breaches of privacy are more likely to be persons with license to get into the certain parts of the system who may browse through client records, or search to see if certain persons are in the system.

Limited access is usually mandated. However, the larger the system, the more accessible the information and the more confidentiality is at risk. The case manager will probably not possess the technological sophistication to address the possibility of unauthorized access from outside the agency, but may be in a position to note persons inside the agency who appear to be accessing screens or reports outside their area of responsibility. Like any breach of ethics, these incidents should be reported to the administration.

Client Rights

While each agency, profession, and program is likely to have guidelines on the ethical treatment and rights of their clients, there are several that are usually found in human service agencies. Whether or not they are specifically written into an agency's code of behavior, they serve as a guide for professional behavior for anyone.

Cost of Services

The client has the right to know the cost of services prior to the rendering of the service, especially in cases where the client will be responsible for payment. Cost here can mean more than the immediate payment due; in some cases, accepting one service eliminates qualification for others. Therefore, the case manager should be very explicit on the advantages and disadvantages of every element of the care plan to protect the client.

Change in Service

The client has the right to be notified of any change of service, termination of service, or discharge from the program. This action should occur immediately and with a full explanation. The sooner the client can be notified, the more chance that any error, failure to supply information, or confusion can be corrected so that the stabilized status of the client is not endangered. For clients who suffer cognitive impairment, it is most essential that they understand the withdrawal or change of services. Clients who have been receiving services from the same person at the same time for long periods can be very disrupted, irritated, and confused when any element changes. For very fragile clients, some home health aids who know months in advance of a change in their employment, will discuss the upcoming change at every visit to give the client time to adjust beforehand.

Refusal of Service

In most systems, the client has the right to withdraw from the case management program at any time that the person is dissatisfied with the case management service being given. If the service has been mandated by court order or through a probation or parole system, this is obviously not the case. But those receiving protective, health, or social services have the right to refuse any service or all services. The case manager should express an opinion on the appropriateness of the action, and, if it is felt that the client will be in jeopardy without care, take the matter to the supervisor. In some cases, the client may not be able to make such a decision rationally and other methods of intervention are needed. However, in most cases, the client is competent to understand the consequences of terminating services and such a request must be honored.

CASE EXAMPLE

Donald, case manager for a mental health center, was surprised to receive a call from Andy that he was terminating his case. Andy explained that his older brother was moving to town and would be caring for his personal needs as well as providing daily supervision, so there was no point in staying in the community support program. Donald checked Andy's record, and seeing no record of a brother, decided to investigate. Upon arriving at Andy's house, he discovered a transient, unrelated to Andy, living in the home. Whether Andy developed the illusion on his own or the new "brother" initiated the relationship, Donald was never sure. The visitor decided that he should find other living arrangements and Andy's case was not terminated.

An Appeals Process

Clients have the right to a grievance procedure if they feel their rights have been violated or perceive discrimination or inappropriate treatment. Each agency should have such a procedure in place; it is the obligation of the case manager to become acquainted with the means of appealing a decision and to advise clients about the options available to them.

EXERCISES

1. One of your clients has discovered that another client in the same housing project is getting more services and demands more for herself. How do you handle the situation within the limits of confidentiality?

2. Imagine yourself as a client in a case management program. What type of person would you want as a case manager? Make a list of qualities and rank them by importance.

3. Many professions require licenses or certificates in order to work with the public. Do you think case management should be one of them? What standards would you use for evaluating an applicant?

4. One element of ethics, beneficence, is based on the principle to "do no harm." Another is to support self-determination. Describe a case in which these two elements are not compatible and what considerations the case manager must make.

5. Although you assume he knew that a client has a right to review his case record, the case manager who had Wesley's case before you had entered some disturbing language into the narrative. Wesley was referred to as "nutty as a fruitcake," "a space cadet," and "hopeless." Now you receive a call from Wesley's attorney that he is subpoenaing the record for a probation hearing. What actions do you take?

KEY TERMS

standards
ethics
autonomy
confidentiality

NOTES

1. Quick, B. (1997). The relationship between personality traits and job satisfaction for case managers. *The Journal of Care Management, 3* (5), 78–82
2. Nufer, Y., Rosenberg, H., & Smith, D. H. (1998). Consumer and case manager perceptions of important case manager characteristics. *Journal of Rehabilitation, 64* (4), 40–47.
3. Certification of Insurance Rehabilitation Specialists Commission. (1992). *CCM Certification Guide.*

4. Case Management Standards Work Group. (1992). *NASW standards for social work case management.*

5. General Accounting Office. (1994). *Long-term care reform: States' views on key elements of well-designed programs for the elderly* (HEHS-94-227).

6. Health Care Financing Administration. (1993). *Approaches to quality under home and community-based services waivers.*

7. General Accounting Office. (1994). *Long-term care reform: States' views on key elements of well-designed programs for the elderly* (HEHS-94-227).

8. Abramson, M. (1996). Toward a more holistic understanding of ethics in social work. *Social Work in Health Care, 23* (2), 1–14.

CHAPTER

10 Case Management Populations

As the popularity of the case management function has increased, the numbers and types of populations offered the service have expanded. Originally the domain of elder care and some mental health programs, the premise of having one professional assist the client in dealing with issues of everyday life has found a place in most human services. In most cases the same general types of tasks are performed: outreach, referral, prescreening, assessment, care planning, monitoring, reassessment, and disengagement. However, for each population the degree of client choice, the intensity of the client–case manager relationship, the size of the caseload, and the goals may differ.

The numbers of public and private organizations adding case management to their operations continues to grow and, undoubtedly, the groups to whom the service is available will increase over the next decade. This chapter will offer an assortment of populations and programs that are currently receiving case management to demonstrate its applicability to diverse social and health issues.

Persons with Chronic Disabilities

Undoubtedly, the segment of the population most utilizing case management is those with chronic illnesses. Chronic conditions affect people of all ages and all strata of society, from newborns to octogenarians, and from the very wealthy to the impoverished. And, contrary to a popular misconception, the elderly are not the only ones with chronic and debilitating conditions. Men and women of all ages, ethnicities, education and income levels, and states of health have chronic conditions.

Some chronic conditions are disabling only some of the time; they require episodic care. Chronic conditions do not always get worse; the health status of a person with a chronic condition can improve, deteriorate, or shift in either direction. Certain segments of society are more likely to have and be disabled by a chronic condition than others, notably the old, the poor, and those who have more than one chronic condition.

Chronic care differs substantially from what most people associate with medical care. Medical care uses intensive, hospital-based, often high-technology medical services to cure acute manifestations of a disease or injury. Chronic care seeks to enable people with functional limitations to regain or maintain the highest level of independence and functioning possible. Because chronic conditions by definition cannot be fully cured, chronic care also emphasizes long-term assistance and compassionate care.

The Elderly

Historically, nursing home care has been the primary option for the **elderly** in need of any long-term care services. However, most elderly people strongly prefer to remain in their homes and receive services in the community. Because in-home and community-based care are generally less expensive than nursing home care, expenditures for long-term care services can be contained to the extent that services can be provided in the home. Consequently, there has been a gradual expansion of in-home and community-based long-term care.

However, these programs have grown in a fragmented fashion with varying eligibility requirements and they often are administered by different state agencies. As a result, elderly people may have difficulty locating and obtaining the services they need. It has also been shown that a person can age successfully even though there are physical limitations if they have interactions with others, a sense of purpose, autonomy, personal growth, and self-acceptance.[1] Case management programs for seniors therefore work to promote a positive self-image and better ability to cope with disabilities.

HIV/AIDS Patients

A number of community-based programs have targeted persons with **HIV/AIDS** and their caregivers. People with AIDS (acquired immunodeficiency syndrome) were experiencing extreme difficulty in gaining access to public and private services because of the providers' fear of contagion. Initially, the limited number of services coupled with societal prejudice created hardships for this population. Clients avoided potential rejection by isolating themselves or relying on informal resources for care. Small community-based agencies targeted to AIDs patients were unable to meet the demand for services. Additionally, insurance companies were unwilling to assume the cost of care, further reducing opportunities for services.

Local organizations instituted case management to assist the client and caregiver in locating and using supportive services. These programs found that offering this type of assistance positively influenced service use and a change in service use over time, highlighting the importance of case management as a mechanism for integrating informal and formal care and demonstrating that service utilization is influenced by the social context of illness.[2] For some communities, the solution was the establishment of a local case management program that focused on advocacy and service coordination. One such project in Los Angeles included an insurance counselor on the case management team.[3]

Case management for AIDS patients takes characteristics from several other targeted groups. Like case managers for the mentally ill, working with the AIDS population requires a knowledge of community services, an awareness of psychosocial issues of drug use, sexual behavior, poverty, and discrimination. In addition, knowledge of community-based health services such as hospice care is shared with those case managers who deal with a frail elderly caseload.[4]

Programs for AIDS patients vary in the skill level of services they offer directly. A program may provide home health care, food vouchers, transportation for medical treatment, financial assistance for rent, or certain medical supplies. Targeting may be specific such as a program for pediatric AIDS patients with special issues like drug-addicted mothers, families with no resources and lack of foster care, and people of color with special needs who have AIDS.[5]

Unwed/Teenage Mothers

Although the nation's infant mortality rate continues to decline, the most recent data available ranks the United States twenty-second among nations in infant mortality and twenty-first in low birth weight. Under Medicaid, many states have instituted new programs to improve women's access to medical prenatal care and enhance prenatal care services. Those states that included a case management component in their programs had better outcomes in birth weight and infant mortality than those states that did not.[6]

High-risk pregnancies are defined as those with factors of poverty, medical risk, teen pregnancy, and stressful work conditions. Case management to this population can offer services such as resolution of stress and grief through offering support, improved living conditions, including both physical housing and family problems, empowering women to seek appropriate social and familial support, substance abuse treatment when needed, early and continuous prenatal care, infant care, and parenting skills.[7]

Having disrupted her education, the teenage mother may never attain the diploma that the labor market increasingly demands, even for low-wage jobs. Women who begin childbearing during their teenage years are significantly more likely than women who postpone having children to live in poverty, to receive public assistance, and to have long periods of welfare dependency. Communities throughout the country have responded to the growth in the number of disadvantaged unwed teenage mothers by creating a diverse range of programs aimed at helping them move toward economic self-sufficiency—in particular, to obtain a high school diploma or General Educational Development certificate (GED). A Government Accounting Office (GAO) study of programs for **unwed/teenage mothers** discovered that intensive case management, in addition to monitoring school attendance, helped resolve participants' problems that were identified through monitoring. Case managers offered assistance, such as counseling, on-site child care, or, for more specialized needs, help in accessing the appropriate resources.[8]

Mental Health Clients

An important function of any case manager is crisis intervention; for those with a **mental health** caseload, this is sometimes the primary function. The adjustment to community living made by many formerly institutionalized psychiatric patients is quite tenuous. Significant crises may be precipitated by unexpected changes in the environment, even events that seem trivial to persons with normal coping ability. If such crises are not managed in a timely fashion, they can easily lead to deterioration of the patient's level of functioning and perhaps to rehospitalization. The case manager's job includes being available to both patients and their families in times of crisis and being capable of either providing or linking them to needed crisis intervention supports.[9]

Veterans

The Veterans Administration's programs employ case management to ensure coordination of the services needed by and provided to a patient. In this program, nurses are usually the primary case managers. Case management may address only a veteran's health needs or the total needs of a veteran and his or her family. Similarly, case management may be limited to the process of arranging initial services or may be an ongoing process for the duration of an illness. Not everyone discharged to home health care from a hospital is given case management; some **veterans** and their families may act as their own case managers. When case management is appropriate, it is seen as important to the adequacy of the home health care veterans receive. In a GAO study, 68 percent of the questionnaire respondents said that case management greatly improves the adequacy of care patients receive.[10]

The Developmentally Disabled

The majority of persons with **developmental disabilities** live with their families, usually with their parents until the parents' death or disability and then either with a sibling or institutional placement. Even when an adult with developmental disabilities lives in an out-of-home placement such as a group home, siblings often maintain a close relationship with him or her.[11]

A relatively new population needing case management is the developmentally disabled elderly. Once the family support structure has diminished or dissolved entirely, a group which had always needed care, now intensified by old age, becomes critically at risk. The good news is that they may be eligible for assistance from both the aging network and the developmental disabilities service system; the bad news is that this requires even more coordination.

Child Abuse

Parents' inability to cope with stress is seen as a major cause of child abuse and neglect. Using case management to intervene in high-risk cases, such as families in poverty, focuses on handling environmental problems to reduce the stress. In some systems, the case manager may also be a child protective service worker with the authority to seek legal action such as removal from the home. In other organizations, foster care case managers supervise children who have been removed from their homes and provide case management services to parents with the goal of reuniting the family.[12]

Case management may also be used as an alternative to foster care. A program designed for the families of children with serious emotional disturbance (SED) provided intensive case management while allowing the child to stay in his home. Staffed by a case manager and parent advocate, services like respite care, flexible service money, parent support groups, and behavior management skills training are offered.[13]

School Children

School social workers are another group utilizing case management techniques. As an early warning system for child abuse, they can often identify troubled families at an early stage and offer assistance in a nonthreatening way. They are also well placed to identify and counsel academically troubled students. Case management is a time-effective, flexible system that allows a collaborative team to monitor and coordinate care for monitoring, evaluating, and recording academic achievements of referred at-risk students.[14]

Substance Abuse

Case management has proved to be effective in assisting those with alcohol or drug abuse. Although case managed clients in one study had a higher drug severity score than non–case managed clients, they were more likely to remain in treatment long enough to reach a length of stay associated with more successful treatment and less likely to be admitted to detox within ninety days of discharge.[15]

For clients under criminal justice supervision in the community, case management may also have monitoring and reporting functions. In such a scheme, the case manager is obligated to report noncompliance to criminal justice authorities who then decide whether to change the terms of supervision or to apply sanctions. Case management for crime-involved drug users is designed mainly to reduce further drug use and crime but may also promote reductions in HIV risk behavior. One study found a favorable effect on the frequency of unprotected sex and on the frequency of sex while high.[16] In fact, a different study determined that substance abusers who received only case management services demonstrated similar outcomes to those who received both case management and conventional services, suggesting that case management services may be a useful alternative.[17]

EXERCISES

1. Complete the following chart with specific tasks a case manager might perform with each of the client populations.

	Outreach	Assessment	Monitoring
Elderly			
Teenage Mothers			
AIDS			
Child Abuse			
IV-drug Users			
Learning Impaired School Children			
Non-English Speaking Immigrants			

KEY TERMS

elderly
substance abusers
HIV/AIDS
unwed/teenage mothers
mental health
veterans
developmental disabilities

NOTES

1. Fisher, B. J. (1995). Successful aging, life satisfaction, and generativity in later life. *International Journal of Aging and Human Development, 41* (3), 239–250.

2. London, A. S., & LeBlanc, A. J. (1998). The integration of informal care, case management and community-based services for persons with HIV/AIDS. *AIDS Care, 10* (4), 481–503.

3. Sonsel, G., Paradise, F., & Stroup, S. (1988). Case-management practice in an AIDS service organization. *Social Casework: Journal of Contemporary Social Work, 69,* 388–92.

4. Peitte, J., & Fleishman, J. A. (1992). The structure and process of AIDS case management. *Health & Social Work, 17* (1), 47–57.

5. Kerson, T. S. (1991). Contra Costa County AIDS case management program. *Health & Social Work, 16* (2), 142–144.

6. Government Accounting Office. (1994). *Medicaid prenatal care: States improve access and enhance services, but face new challenges* (Briefing Report, 05/10/94, GAO/HEHS-94-152BR).

7. Gonzalez-Calvo, J., & Jackson, J. (1998). Psychosocial factors and birth outcome: African American women in case management. *Journal of Health Care for the Poor & Underserved, 9* (4), 395–420.

8. Government Accounting Office. *Welfare to work: Approaches that help teenage mothers complete high school.* (Letter Report, 09/29/95, GAO/HEHS/PEMD-95-202).

9. Intagliata, J., Willer, B., & Egri, G. (1988). The role of the family in delievering case management services. In M. Harris and L. Bachrach (Eds.), *Clinical case management.* San Francisco: Jossey-Bass.

10. Government Accounting Office. *Veterans' health care: VA's approaches to meeting veterans' home health care needs* (Letter Report, 03/15/96, GAO/HEHS-96-68).

11. Seltzer, M. M. (1992). Training families to be case managers for elders with developmental disabilities. *Generations, 16* (1), 65–71.

12. Ballew, J., & Mink, G. (1996). *Case management in social work: Developing the professional skills needed for work with multiproblem clients.* Springfield, IL: Charles C. Thomas.

13. Evans, M. E., & Armstrong, M. I. (1994). Development and evaluation of treatment foster care and family-centered intensive case management in New York. *Journal of Emotional & Behavioral Disorders, 2* (4), 228–240.

14. Shepard-Tew, D., & Creamer, D. A. (1998). Elementary school integrated services teams: Applying case-management techniques. *Professional School Counseling, 2* (2), 141–146.

15. Shwartz, M., & Baker, G. (1997). Improving publicly funded substance abuse treatment: The value of case management. *American Journal of Public Health, 87* (10), 1659–65.

16. Longshore, D., & Turner, S. (1998). Effects of case management on drug user's risky sex. *Prison Journal, 78* (1), 6–31.

17. Siegal, H. A., & Rapp, R. C. (1997). The role of case management in retaining clients in substance abuse treatment: An exploratory analysis. *Journal of Drug Issues, 27* (4), 821–832.

GLOSSARY

activity limitation   A long-term reduction in a person's capacity to perform the average kind or amount of activities appropriate to the person's age group such as going to school, going to work, and living independently.

administrative authority   Based on policies and procedures from legal contracts or interagency agreements that specify the right of the case manager to authorize, monitor, and terminate services.

assessment   Process by which the health, functional, social, psychological, cognitive, financial, environmental, and support needs of a client are identified utilizing a structured assessment instrument.

breadth of service   Refers to the scope of the client's problems that will be addressed through a structured and comprehensive assessment and care plan process.

brokerage model   The case manager serves as a broker or arranger of services.

case management   An interdisciplinary service designed to facilitate linkage to other services through a direct relationship between a case manager and client that is usually long term.

chronic illness   The presence of long-term disease or symptoms, commonly a duration of three months or longer.

client   The recipient of services.

developmental disabilities   A broad range of conditions evident at birth or in early childhood that can result in lifelong deficits in mental, psychosocial, and physical functioning.

disability   A limitation or inability to perform socially defined activities and roles expected of individuals in the manner considered normal resulting from impairment or chronic illness.

disengagement   The closing of a case is a process of gradual or sudden withdrawal of services, as the situation indicates, on a planned basis.

duration   How long the case manager is involved with the client performing, monitoring, and reevaluating to adjust care, rather than just collecting data for tracking purposes.

fiscal authority   Gives the case manager control over funding used to purchase services, either for the client, for a caseload, or for all the clients of an agency.

functional limitations   Resulting from impairment or chronic illness, this is a restriction or lack of ability to perform an action or activity in the manner or within the range considered normal.

generalist case manager   A case management system in which one individual has responsibility for being the single source of service contact related to serving a given client.

impairment   A physiological, psychological, or anatomical abnormality of bodily structure or function; includes losses or abnormalities, not just those attributable to active pathology.

intensity   Refers to the amount of time the case manager has to spend with each client based on caseload size.

interview   A form of communication in which information is exchanged.

joint funding authority   Two or more agencies are given resources to provide services under an interagency program.

legal authority   A legislative mandate that designates an organization responsible for a particular service or a particular population.

managed care model   The case management organization is at risk for all long-term care services, therefore the incentive for appropriate case finding and management is increased.

medical care   Intensive, hospital-based, often high-technology medical services to cure acute manifestations of a disease or injury.

monitoring   Process through which the case manager maintains contact on a regular basis with the client, the family, and the providers of service in order to ensure that the services are appropriate and meeting the individual client's current needs.

outcome indicators   Information used to judge the result of care.

outreach   A process of creating an awareness in the professional community and in the general public of the availability of services in order to identify and establish contact with those who are appropriate for case management services.

payers   Those agencies or companies that incur financial outlays so that the client will receive services.

plan of care   A statement of goals to meet the client's needs and identification of services necessary to achieve these goals.

prescreening   A process through which the person's need for case management is evaluated.

primary care model   A case management system in which the physician acts as the case manager.

process indicators   Judgement of quality by assessing the activities which took place.

provider   An individual or organization that delivers a service to clients.

reassessment   Process whereby client status, function, and outcomes are reviewed according to an established time frame.

referral   A process through which various persons in the community in need of case management are referred to the program.

secondary conditions   Conditions related to the main illness or impairment that further diminish the person's quality of life, threaten health, or increase vulnerability to further disability.

service coordination   Process through which the case manager arranges and/or authorizes services and implements the service plan using various providers necessary to meet the client's needs.

service management model   Case managers perform as managers with the primary charge of getting work done through others.

specialist case manager   A case management system in which a client is assigned several different case managers, depending on the needs and services reflected by the assessment.

specialist–generalist model   A case management system in which a client is assigned a single case manager who performs multiple tasks as in the generalist model. The specialist–generalist may be trained in a particular discipline.

structural measures   Used to judge the quality of an administrative system such as the number of clients, qualifications of case managers, and in-home workers and client turnover.

therapist–case manager   A case management system in which the case managers provide a degree of clinical care.

REFERENCES

Abramson, M. (1996). Toward a more holistic understanding of ethics in social work. *Social Work in Health Care, 23* (2), 1–14.

Alzheimer's Association. (1991). *Time out! The case for a national family caregiver support policy.* Chicago: Alzheimer's Association.

American Association of Retired Persons. (1997). Managed care: A consumer's guide. [Online] AARP WebPlace, www.aarp.org.

Auslander, G., & Litwin, H. (1991). Correlates of social worker contact with client's family networks. *Journal of Social Service Research, 14* (1/2), 147–165.

Austin, C. (1993). Case management: A systems perspective. *Families in Society, 74* (8) pp. 451–459

Austin, C. (1992). Case management in long term care. In S. M. Rose (Ed.), *Case management & social work practice.* (pp. 199–218). New York: Longman.

Ballew. J., & Mink, G. (1996). *Case management in social work.* Springfield, IL: Charles C. Thomas.

Barling, J., MacEwen, K. E., Kelloway, E. K., & Higginbottom, S. F. (1994). Predictors and outcomes of elder-care-based interrole conflict. *Psychology and Aging, 9* (3), 391–397.

Bissell, G. (1996). Personal ethics in social work with older people. *International Social Work, 39,* 257–263.

Case Management Standards Work Group. (1992). *NASW standards for social work case management.*

Certification of Insurance Rehabilitation Specialists Commission. (1992). *CCM certification guide.* Rolling Meadows, IL: Commission on Case Manager Certification.

Cicirelli, V. G., Coward, R. T., & Dwyer, J. W. (1992). Siblings as caregivers for impaired elders. *Research on Aging, 14* (3), 331–350.

Davidson, G. B., & Penrod, J. (1991). Modeling the costs of case management in long-term care. *Health Care Financing Review, 13* (1), 73–82.

Dinerman, M. (1992). Managing the maze: Case management and service delivery. *Administration in Social Work, 16* (1), 1–9.

Douville, M. L. (1993). Case management: Predicting activity patterns. *Journal of Gerontological Social Work, 20* (3/4), 43–55.

Dwyer, J. W., & Coward, R. T. (1991). A multivariate comparison of the involvement of adult sons versus daughters in the care of impaired parents. *Journal of Gerontology: Social Sciences, 46* (5), S259–269.

Evans, M. E., & Armstrong, M. I. (1994). Development and evaluation of treatment foster care and family-centered intensive case management in New York. *Journal of Emotional & Behavioral Disorders, 2* (4), 228–240.

Feinberg, L. F. (1995). Private sorrows/public issues: The needs of family caregivers. *Journal of Mental Health and Aging, 1,* 213–219.

Fisher, B. J. (1995). Successful aging, life satisfaction, and generativity in later life. *International Journal of Aging and Human Development, 41* (3), 239–250.

Fralich, J., Riley, T., Mollica, R., et al. (1995). *Reducing the cost of institutional care: Downsizing, diversion, closing and conversion of nursing homes.* Portland, ME: National Academy of State Health Policy.

General Accounting Office. (1993). *Long term care case management: State experiences and implications for federal policy.* Washington, DC: U.S. Government Printing Office.

General Accounting Office. (1994). *Long-term care: Status of quality assurance and measurement in home and community-based services.* (Letter Report, 03/31/94, GAO/PEMD-94-19). Washington, DC: U.S. Government Printing Office.

General Accounting Office. (1994). *Long-term care reform: States views on key elements of well-designed programs for the elderly.* [HEHS-94-227] Washington, DC: U.S. Government Printing Office.

Government Accounting Office. (1994). *Medicaid prenatal care: States improve access and enhance services, but face new challenges.* (Briefing Report, 05/10/94, GAO/HEHS-94-152BR). Washington, DC: U.S. Government Printing Office.

Government Accounting Office. *Welfare to work: Approaches that help teenage mothers complete high school.* (Letter Report, 09/29/95, GAO/HEHS/PEMD-95-202). Washington, DC: U.S. Government Printing Office.

Government Accounting Office. *Veterans' health care: VA's approaches to meeting veterans' home health care needs.* (Letter Report, 03/15/96, GAO/HEHS-96-68). Washington, DC: U.S. Government Printing Office.

Gonzalez-Calvo, J., & Jackson, J. (1998). Psychosocial factors and birth outcome: African American women in case management. *Journal of Health Care for the Poor & Underserved, 9* (4), 395–420.

Gorey, K. M., Rice, R. W., & Brice, G. C. (1992). The prevalence of elder care responsibilities among the work force population. *Research on Aging, 14* (3), 399–418.

Health Care Financing Administration. (1993). *Approaches to quality under home and community-based services waivers.* Baltimore: HCFA.

Heus, M., & Pincus, A. (1986). *The creative generalist: A guide to social work practice.* Barneveld, WI: Micamar Publishing.

Himes, C. (1994). Parental caregiving by adult women. *Research on Aging, 16* (2), 191–211.

Intagliata, J., Willer, B., & Egri, G. (1988). The role of the family in delivering case management services. In M. Harris and L. Bachrach (Eds.), *Clinical case management.* San Francisco: Jossey-Bass.

Kerson, T. S. (1991). Contra Costa County AIDS case management program. *Health & Social Work, 16* (2), 142–144.

Lechner, V. M. (1993). Racial group responses to work and parent care. *Families in Society: The Journal of Contemporary Human Services, 74* (2), 93–103.

Lee, G. R., Dwyer, J. W., & Coward, R. T. (1993). Gender differences in parent care: Demographic factors and same-gender preferences. *Journal of Gerontology: Social Sciences, 48* (4), S9–16.

Locke, B., Garrison, R., & Winship, J. (1998). *Generalist social work practice: Context, story and partnerships.* Pacific Grove, CA: Brooks/Cole Publishing Company.

London, A. S., & LeBlanc, A. J. (1998). The integration of informal care, case management and community-based services for persons with HIV/AIDS. *AIDS Care, 10* (4), 481–503.

Longshore, D., & Turner, S. (1998). Effects of case management on drug user's risky sex. *Prison Journal, 78* (1), 6–31.

Loring, M. T., & Wimberly, E. T. (1993). The time-limited hot line. *Social Work, 38* (3), 344–347.

Merrit, J., & Neugeboren, B. (1990). Factors affecting agency capacity for inter-organizational coordination. *Administration in Social Work, 14* (4), 73–85.

Morrow-Howell, N. (1992). Clinical case management: The hallmark of gerontological social work. *Journal of Gerontological Social Work, 3–4*, 119–31.

Moxely, D. P. (1997). *Case management by design.* Chicago: Nelson-Hall Publishers.

National Alliance for Caregiving and the American Association of Retired Persons. (1997). *Family caregiving in the U.S.—Findings from a national survey.* Bethesda: National Alliance for Caregiving.

Newcomer, R., & Arnsberger, P. (1997). Case management, client risk factors, and service use. *Health Care Financing Review, 19* (1), 105–121.

Nishimoto, R., Weil, M., & Thiel, K. S. (1991). A service tracking and referral form to monitor the receipt of services in a case management program. *Administration in Social Work, 15* (3), 33–47.

Nufer, Y., Rosenberg, H., & Smith, D. H. (1998). Consumer and case manager perceptions of important case manager characteristics. *Journal of Rehabilitation, 64* (4), 40–47.

Pearlman, D. N., & Crown, W. H. (1992). Alternative sources of social support and their impacts on institutional risk. *The Gerontologist, 32* (4), 527–535.

Peitte, J., & Fleishman, J. A. (1992). The structure and process of AIDS case management. *Health & Social Work, 17* (1), 47–57.

Quick, B. (1997). The relationship between personality traits and job satisfaction for case managers. *The Journal of Care Management, 3* (5), 78–82.

Ramsdell, J. (1991). Geriatric assessment in the home. *Clinics in Geriatric Medicine, 7* (4), 677–693.

Roberts-DeGennaro, M. (1987). Developing case management as a practice model. *Social Casework: Journal of Contemporary Social Work, 68*, 466–70.

Robinson, K. M. (1997). The family's role in long-term care. *Journal of Gerontology Nursing, 23* (9), 7–11.

Rose, S. (1992). *Case management & social work practice.* New York: Longman.

Rothman, J., & Sager, J. S. (1998). *Case management: Integrating individual and community practice.* Boston: Allyn and Bacon.

Rothman, J. (1992). *Guidelines for case management: Putting research to professional use.* Itasca, IL: F. E. Peacock Publishers.

Rubin, A. (1992). Case management. In S. M. Rose (Ed.), *Case Management & Social Work Practice.* New York: Longman.

Seltzer, M. M. (1992). Training families to be case managers for elders with developmental disabilities. *Generations, 16* (1), 65–71.

Shepard-Tew, D., & Creamer, D. A. (1998). Elementary school integrated services teams: Applying case-management techniques. *Professional School Counseling, 2* (2), 141–146.

Shwartz, M., & Baker, G. (1997). Improving publicly funded substance abuse treatment: The value of case management. *American Journal of Public Health, 87* (10), 1659–65.

Siegal, H. A., & Rapp, R. C. (1997). The role of case management in retaining clients in substance abuse treatment: An exploratory analysis. *Journal of Drug Issues, 27* (4), 821–832.

Sonsel, G., Paradise, F., & Stroup, S. (1988). Case-management practice in an AIDS service organization. *Social Casework: Journal of Contemporary Social Work, 69*, 388–92.

Steinberg, J. A., & St. Coeur, M. (1996). *Case management practice guidelines.* St. Louis: Mosby.

Steinberg, R., & Carter, G. (1983). *Case management and the elderly.* Lexington, MA: Lexington Books.

Suitor, J. J., & Pillemer, K. (1993). Support and interpersonal stress in the social networks of married daughters caring for parents with dementia. *Journal of Gerontology: Social Sciences, 48* (1), S1–8.

Topinkova, E. (1994). Care for elders with chronic disease and disability. *Hastings Center Report,* Sept–Oct.

Tower, K. D. (1994). Consumer-centered social work practice: Responding to client self-determination. *Social Work, 39* (2), 191–196.

Valentine, J., & Aguero, L. (1996). Defining the components of street outreach for HIV prevention: The contact and the encounter. *Public Health Reports, 111* (1), 68–74.

Walrop, D., & Taylor, N. D. (1994). A community hospitals role in lowering infant rates through a maternal access-to-care program. *Health & Social Work, 19* (2), 148–153.

Wells, L. M., & Schachter, B. (1993). Enhancing rehabilitation through mutual aid: Outreach to people with recent amputations. *Health & Social Work, 18* (3), 221–229.

Wolk, J. L., Sullivan, W. P., & Hartmann, D. J. (1994). The managerial nature of case management. *Social Work, 39* (2), 152–160.

Woodside, M., & McClam, T. (1998). *Generalist case management.* Pacific Grove: Brooks/Cole.

INDEX